Mountain and ....

Volume 1

MARA BOOKS

www.marabooks.co.uk
www.northerneyebooks.com

Mountain and Hill Walking in
Snowdonia
Volume 1

Carl Rogers

First published in April 2009 by **Mara Books**, 22 Crosland Terrace, Helsby, Frodsham, Cheshire WA6 9LY.

Telephone: 01928 723744

www.marabooks.co.uk

ISBN 978-1-902512-18-1

Important advice to readers and users of this guide

Whilst every effort has been made to ensure that the information in this book is correct, the author or the publisher can accept no responsibility for errors, loss or injury however caused. Check all details before you proceed. Your use of this book indicates your assumption of the risks involved in mountain walking and scrambling and is an acknowledgement of your own sole responsibility for your safety.

Layout, design, photography and cartography by Carl Rogers
© Carl Rogers 2009

Title page: The Snowdon Horseshoe from Llynnau Mymbyr

British Library Cataloguing-in-publication data.
A catalogue is available for this book from the British Library.

Whilst every effort has been made to ensure that the information in this book is correct, the author or the publisher can accept no responsibility for errors, loss or injury however caused.

Maps based on out of copyright Ordnance Survey mapping

Contents

Introduction 6
List of summits covered by this book in descending altitude 14

The Carneddau 16
1. Northern Carneddau from Aber Falls 22
2. The round of Cwm Caseg & Cwm Llafar 26
3. Cwm Llafar Horseshoe.. 30
4. The Carneddau from the east via Cwm Eigiau 35
5. Southern Carneddau from Ogwen 40
6. Pen Llithrig y Wrach & Pen yr helgi Ddu from Capel Curig 44
7. Craigiau Gleison & the Crafnant skyline 47

The Glyderau 52
8. The Northern Glyderau from Nant Peris 58
9. Elidir Fawr, Foel Goch & Y Garn from Nant Peris 61
10. Glyder Fawr & Y Garn by Y Gribin 64
11. Glyder Fach & Glyder Fawr from Llyn Ogwen 68
12. Glyder Fach & Glyder Fawr from Pen-y-Gwryd 73
13. Senior's Ridge, Glyder Fawr & Y Gribin 77
14. Tryfan via Heather Terrace, the South Ridge & Cwm Tryfan 80
15. Tryfan—East face, South Ridge & Braich Ddeugwm 83
16. The Bochlwyd Horseshoe 87
17. Eastern Glyderau from Capel Curig 93

Snowdon/Yr Wyddfa 98
18. Snowdon from Llanberis—The Llanberis Ridge 106
19. Snowdon from the west—Snowdon Ranger/Rhyd-Ddu Path 110
20. Snowdon from the east—Pyg Track/Miners' Track 114
21. The Snowdon Hourseshoe 118
22. Snowdon from the south—Cwm Llan Horseshoe 124
23. Cwm Glas Horseshoe—Crib Goch/Gyrn Lâs Ridge 130
24. Moel Eilio group 136

The Eifionydd hills 140
25. Mynydd Mawr from Rhyd-Ddu 144
26. Moel Hebog from Beddgelert 147
27. The Nantlle Ridge 151

Introduction

SNOWDONIA IS ONE OF THE MOST CELEBRATED and spectacular highland areas in the British Isles—a region of hills, mountains and wild moorland occupying the northwest corner of Wales. Its name records not just the geography of the area, but also the impression Dark Age Saxon invaders had of these mountains. Snowdon means *'mountains'* or *'hills of snow'* (*snow dun*). Today Snowdon is the name given to just the highest peak in the range, but originally it referred to all the hills and mountains between the estuaries of Afon Dyfi in the south and Afon Conwy in the north—an area covered today by the Snowdonia National Park.

The hills and mountains of Snowdonia will captivate any lover of wild mountain scenery, with around 100 summits (depending on how you define a 'summit') above 2,000 feet (approx. 610 metres). Fourteen of these exceed 3,000 feet (914 metres), of which four raise their heads above 1,000 metres.

The peaks of the Snowdon Horseshoe from Capel Curig

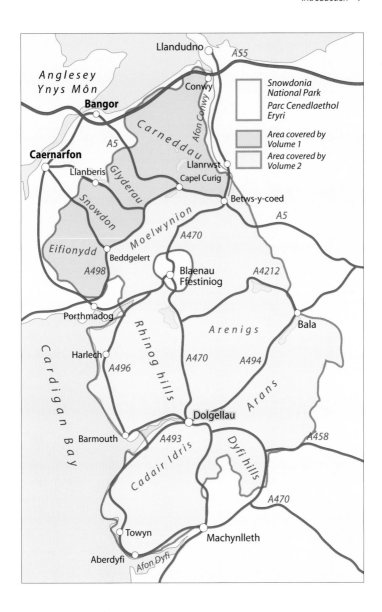

The west face of Tryfan rising above the Ogwen Valley

Despite the relatively small area covered by the National Park—just 80km/50 miles north to south and 40km/25 miles east to west—there is great variety in its hills and mountains. This is due mainly to the underlying geology creating a variety of height, form and flora. The highest and most spectacular peaks are in the north around Snowdon where all the fourteen 3,000-foot summits are to be found. Rocky ridges, high crags and one or two sharp Alpine-like summits make this area the best known, with by far the most visitors.

The central section of the park is the wildest and least known. Much of it is high moorland at around 300 metres with well-spaced summits barely two-thirds the height of Snowdon and its neighbours. Even the names in this wilderness are unfamiliar: Moel Llyfnant, Rhobell Fawr, Llethr. The unusual rocky wilds of the Rhinog hills are also to be found here.

The southern section of the park is better known, mainly on account of Cadair Idris, once thought to be the highest mountain in Wales and famous ever since. The summits here are high and rugged like the north and are graced by wide sea views across Cardigan Bay.

Snowdonia's hills and mountains divide conveniently into distinct groups which are clearly defined, separated from each other by major valleys and quite different in character. From north to south they are the: Carneddau; Glyderau; Snowdon; Eifionydd; Moelwynion; Rhinogydd; Arenig; Arans; Dyfi hills and Cadair Idris. This guide is presented in two volumes with the first four groups being the subject of this first volume and the remaining hill groups covered by volume two.

The most northerly group is the Carneddau, a high plateauland of broad pillowy summits containing the largest area of land above 700 metres in the whole of Wales, including six of Snowdonia's highest 3,000-foot mountains. They cover an area larger than Snowdon and

Yr Elen, one of the most striking peaks in the Carneddau

Y Garn and Mynydd Drws-y-coed at the eastern end of the famous Nantlle Ridge

the adjacent Glyderau combined, but, with no famous summits and far greater distances required to reach the higher tops, they remain less popular and far less crowded.

The most rugged terrain is found on Snowdon and the Glyderau. These peaks have an abundance of rock faces and narrow ridges making them a scrambler's delight, and there are two summits—Crib Goch on Snowdon and Tryfan in the Glyderau—which have the distinction of lying out of bounds to the non-scrambler. These two groups are far more accessible than the Carneddau with the principal summits lying close to, and visible from, main roads. They have been climbed, walked and photographed more than any other mountains in Snowdonia.

The hills of the adjacent group to the west of Snowdon are somewhat dominated by it, being little more than two-thirds its height. The Eifionydd hills are softer, offering fine 'fell walking' rather than rugged mountain walking, although the famous Nantlle Ridge provides one of the best ridge walks in Wales.

The dramatic North Ridge of Tryfam seen from the lower slopes of Pen-yr Ole Wen

The walks

The routes outlined in the following pages are intended as full day-walks over one or more major summits and cover the full circuit, describing both ascent and descent. *Alternative routes and options, where appropriate, are shown in italics.* Almost all the routes are circular and they have been devised to include all the summits of note in each hill group, but do not necessarily visit every 'top' above a certain altitude (such as the Nuttall 2,000-foot summit list). The walks are—in the authors opinion at least—the best circuits in each group. In compiling them I have not felt obliged to avoid well known rounds (such as the Snowdon Horseshoe) but have dealt with each hill group in equal detail outlining both well-known and obscure routes with the aim of presenting a comprehensive and balanced guide.

A note of caution—although the routes outlined in the following pages carry a detailed route description, I have assumed that anyone following them will have the ability to navigate independently of the book using a large scale Ordnance Survey map and compass. (The Ordnance Survey 1:25,000 Explorer map sheet OL17 covers all the walks in this book.) It is important to remember that this is not an optional skill, it is a basic requirement and without it you are not safe to either walk or scramble in the mountain environment. This guide will not help you if you become lost on the mountains, particularly in bad weather or poor visibility.

Spectacular winter conditions on the summit of Glyder Fawr with Snowdon in the background

Tryfan and Glyder Fach from Pen yr helgi Du in stunning winter conditions

It should also be noted that all the routes are intended as summer walks or scrambles in fine, dry conditions. Poor visibility, wind, rain and especially winter conditions with ice and snow, turn the mountains into a very different environment. If you venture onto the hills in these conditions, be sure you are equipped and experienced enough to deal with them. For winter walking in snow and ice conditions, an ice axe and the knowledge of how to use it is a minimum requirement. Suitable clothing is just as essential.

On the routes labelled **SCRAMBLE** you will need to be confident climbing rocks which, although not technically difficult (not graded rock climbs), will still require agility, a steady head and could well be in an exposed position where a fall would be serious or even fatal. Having said that, all the scrambles described are generally completed without the use of ropes and specialist equipment in normal conditions, ie. dry, summer weather with good visibility and free from snow and ice. If you are in any doubt about the above, avoid these routes until you have more experience. All the scrambles become serious winter climbs under ice and snow and are beyond the scope of this guide.

List of summits covered by this book in descending altitude

Peak	Group	Height	Routes
Snowdon (Yr Wyddfa)	*Snowdon*	1085m/3,560ft	18, 19, 20, 21, 22
Crib y Ddysgl	*Snowdon*	1065m/3,494ft	18, 21, 23
Carnedd Llewelyn	*Carneddau*	1064m/3,490ft	2, 3, 4, 5
Carnedd Dafydd	*Carneddau*	1044m/3,426ft	2, 3, 5
Glyder Fawr	*Glyderau*	999m/3,277ft	10, 11, 12, 13
Glyder Fach	*Glyderau*	994m/3,261ft	11, 12, 16
Pen-yr Ole Wen	*Carneddau*	978m/3,208ft	5
Foel Grach	*Carneddau*	976m/3,202ft	2, 4
Yr Elen	*Carneddau*	962m/3,156ft	3, 5
Y Garn	*Glyderau*	947m/3,104ft	9, 10
Foel Fras	*Carneddau*	942m/3,091ft	1
Carnedd Uchaf	*Carneddau*	926m/3,038ft	1, 2
Elidir Fawr	*Glyderau*	924m/3,031ft	8, 9
Crib Goch	*Snowdon*	923m/3,028ft	21, 23
Tryfan	*Glyderau*	915m/3,010ft	14, 15, 16
Y Lliwedd	*Snowdon*	898m/2,946ft	21, 22
Pen yr Helgi Du	*Carneddau*	833m/2,733ft	5, 6
Foel Goch	*Glyderau*	831m/2726ft	9
Carnedd y Filiast	*Glyderau*	821m/2,693ft	8
Mynydd Perfedd	*Glyderau*	812m/2,664ft	8
Bera Bach	*Carneddau*	807m/2,648ft	1
Y Foel Goch	*Glyderau*	805m/2,641ft	17
Pen Llithrig y Wrach	*Carneddau*	799m/2,621ft	6
Moel Hebog	*Eifionydd hills*	782m/2,565ft	26
Drum	*Carneddau*	770m/2,526ft	1
Gallt yr Ogof	*Glyderau*	763m/2,499ft	17
Drosgl	*Carneddau*	758m/2,487ft	1
Yr Aran	*Snowdon*	747m/2,450ft	22
Craig Cwm Silyn	*Eifionydd hills*	734m/2,408ft	27
Moel Eilio	*Snowdon*	726m/2,382ft	24
Trum y Ddysgl	*Eifionydd hills*	709m/2,326ft	27
Mynydd Mawr	*Eifionydd hills*	698m/2,290ft	25
Mynydd Drws-y-coed	*Eifionydd hills*	695m/2,280ft	27
Creigiau Gleision	*Carneddau*	678m/2,224ft	7
Moel Cynghorion	*Snowdon*	674m/2,211ft	18, 24
Moel yr Ogof	*Eifionydd hills*	655m/2,149ft	26
Mynydd Tal-y-mignedd	*Eifionydd hills*	653m/2,148ft	27
Moel Lefn	*Eifionydd hills*	638m/2,093ft	26
Y Garn	*Eifionydd hills*	633m/2,077ft	27
Foel Gron	*Snowdon*	629m/2,064ft	24
Gallt y Wenallt	*Snowdon*	619m/2,031ft	22
Foel Goch	*Snowdon*	605m/1,985ft	24

Yr Elen rising above Cwm Caseg

The Carneddau

Carnedd Llewelyn and Yr Elen from the northwest

The Carneddau

THE CARNEDDAU ARE SNOWDONIA'S northern-most mountain group—a high, bulky plateauland containing the greatest extent of high ground in the whole of Wales and almost half of Snowdonia's elite 3,000-foot summits—six in all. Covering an area larger than Snowdon and the adjacent Glyderau combined, the Carneddau are broad, stocky mountains having height and stature, but lacking the graceful outlines of their better known neighbours. As a result they are the least know of Snowdonia's high mountains.

The northern summits rise abruptly from the narrow coastal plain which runs between Conwy and Bangor and enjoy wide views out across the Isle of Anglesey and along the North Wales coast towards Cheshire and Lancashire. The deep trough of Dyffryn Conwy defines the eastern limit of the range and the famous Nant Ffrancon forms its western boundary. To the south the heights fall away to the A5 through the Ogwen valley and beside Afon Llugwy. The main summits of the

group are arranged along a broad central ridge running from Bwlch y Ddeufaen in the northeast to Pen-yr Ole Wen above Llyn Ogwen in the southwest. Either side of this main watershed sub ridges and valleys radiate to all points of the compass like the spokes of a giant wheel.

Unlike Snowdon and the adjacent Glyderau—whose high tops consist mainly of narrow ridges and sharp summits—the Carneddau are broad and rounded. Their bulky summits stand well apart from each other connected by high pillowy ridges and separated by deep, dark glacial cwms. Rock faces are in shorter supply here than on nearby Snowdon and the Glyder, but where they do occur they come on a massive scale. The dark precipice of Ysgolion Duon—better known as the 'Black Ladders'—rises almost 300 metres at the head of Cwm Llafar, whilst Craig yr Ysfa, even higher though less steep, guards the head of the remote Cwm Eigiau.

The height and bulk of the Carneddau also means that they both catch and hold more snow than any other summits in Snowdonia. In some ways it is under winter conditions that these mountains really

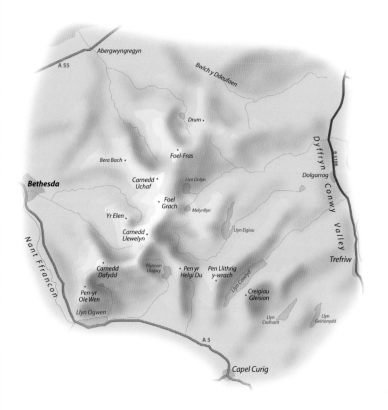

come into their own. If Snowdonia received enough snow for skiing (and occasionally it does) this would be the place for it. The broad featureless summits and high ridges take on a very different feel under winter conditions. It is a pity that such conditions are becoming increasingly rare.

If you have already explored Snowdon and the Glyderau, the Carneddau is the place to make big, new discoveries—like the northeast ridge of Yr Elen, the fine airy scramble on the Llech Ddu Spur, or the

Traversing the ridge between Pen-yr Ole Wen and Carnedd Dafydd

Looking down Cwm Eigiau from Carnedd Llewelyn's east ridge

vast Scottish-like valley of Cwm Eigiau. Though not as spectacular as their counterparts on Snowdon or the Glyderau, you will none-the-less be surprised that these routes are not equally as famous. But the Carneddau hide their secrets well—much of the range is barely visible from the road and there are no classic views of the main summits (such as the view of the Snowdon Horseshoe from Capel Curig, or the east face Tryfan from the A5) to draw the crowds.

The most popular access points are from the Ogwen valley in the south where the main summits can be accessed by the shortest routes. The two main approaches are via the southeast ridge of Pen-yr Ole Wen (the southwest ridge which rises from the western end of Llyn Ogwen is one of the toughest ascents in Snowdonia and in the author's opinion is best avoided) from the eastern end of Llyn Ogwen and the reservoir road which gives rapid (if boring) access to Cwm Llugwy. Both these approaches give access to the main ridge which links all the high tops.

From the west Bethesda provides the best base, situated on the lip of the vast twin valleys of Cwm Caseg and Cwm Llafar. From here Carnedd Dafydd's northwest ridge provides a long tiring approach, whilst the long northern arm of Cwm Caseg gives a longer but easier route onto the main ridge. From the north the Aber Falls provide the best approach but routes form here start almost from sea level and require the greatest height gain of all Snowdonia's mountain walks.

The upper reaches of Cwm Llafar below the northern cliffs of Carnedd Dafydd

Below the Aber Falls

1. Northern Carneddau from Aber Falls

Outline: *A long approach via lanes and Landrover tracks to gain the main Carnedd ridge is followed by easier walking on the high plateau with the option of taking in several summits, including Carnedd Llewelyn, the highest point in the Carneddau. A long but easy descent over broad grassy ridges with superb views and a visit to one of Snowdonia's most spectacular waterfalls.*

Distance: *25km/15½ miles.*

Height gained: *1,400m/4,600ft.*

Summits: *Drum, Foel Fras, Carnedd Uchaf & Bera Bach (Foel Grach and Carnedd Llewelyn optional).*

Starting point: *Begin at the car park for the Aber Falls at Bont Newydd, reached by taking the old lane south from the A55 at Abergwyngregyn. Park just before the bridge.*
Grid ref: SH 662 720.

THE NORTHERN EDGE OF THE CARNEDDAU is very different to the southern half of the group. The broad, gently curving ridges and flat summits which characterise the Carneddau are exaggerated here into expanses of grass and fine stones miles wide. There are no cliff-edged cwms or ankle-bending boulders to negotiate making it ideal walking country. Almost the only rocks encountered are the strange Dartmoor-like tors marking the occasional summit.

The following route begins at near Abergwyngregyn and uses the old Roman road to gain height quickly and access the main Carnedd ridge at Drum. From here, all the northern peaks in the group can be completed in a high-level ridge walk with only minimal height loss between each top. Foel Grach and Carnedd Llewelyn—the highest summit in the group—can be included by an out-and-back walk of

about 5km/3 miles. The rounded northwest ridge of Garnedd Uchaf provides a fine easy descent with superb views in clear weather and you will finish beside one of the most famous and spectacular waterfalls in Wales—the Aber Falls.

The route: Don't follow the obvious footpath to the Aber Falls, cross the bridge and continue along the rising lane for about 1.5km/1 mile to the little parking area where the tarmac ends. The lane continues from here as a rough Landrover track—originally an ancient highway over the mountains to Rowen in the Conwy Valley. Follow this track as it climbs steadily, before contouring the northern slopes of Foel-ganol.

Almost due north of Yr Orsedd there is a junction with a crossing track at GR. 693 722. Turn right here and follow the track over the ridge

On the broad ridge between Carnedd Uchaf and Bera Bach

between Pen Bryn-du and Drosgl with views right to Llyn Anafon. The path/track now curves up the rounded ridge to the summit of Drum.

From Drum the path ahead is clear along the rounded grass ridge to Foel Fras and Garnedd Uchaf.

(Between these two tops a shortcut could be made northwest down Cwm yr Afon Goch which will lead to the top of the Aber Falls. After the initial indistinct slopes, a path establishes itself on the north side of the stream which cascades over rock slabs and into tiny gorges forming pools large and inviting enough to tempt a dip on a hot day. Immediately above the falls the path needs care in one or two places where a slip could be nasty. A zig-zag path takes you down to the bottom of the falls and the car park lies just 2km/1¼ miles along an easy track. This is not recommended in poor visibility.)

(From Garnedd Uchaf you could extend the walk to include Foel Grach and Carnedd Llewelyn by following the good path south along the broad ridge—an out-and-back walk of around 2km/1¼ miles for Foel Grach and 5km/3 miles for Carnedd Llewelyn.)

From Garnedd Uchaf faint paths head northwest down the rounded grass ridge to the castellated top of Yr Aryg and then Bera Bach, or, if you are approaching from the out-and-back extension to Foel Grach or Carnedd Llewelyn, a path contours northwest from the bwlch immediately south of Garnedd Uchaf to join the ridge at Bera Bach.

There are dramatic views from this ridge across the Caseg and Llafar valleys to the slopes of Yr Elen and Carnedd Dafydd.

From Bera Bach a path continues to the south of Drosgl and forks on the bwlch before Gyrn Wigau. Turn right with the main path—now a rough Landrover track—and follow this down to the broad grass bwlch separating the little pyramid of Gyrn and Moel Wnion from Drosgl. Almost at the lowest point bear right, soon picking up a faint path which makes its way beside a stream. This deepens into a small gorge and lower down is crag-lined on the far side.

At a crossing path (North Wales Path) turn right and make your way past Rhaeadr Bach and Rhaeadr Fawr (Aber Falls). Cross a footbridge at Rhaeadr Fawr and follow the path/track north back down the valley to Bont Newydd to return to the car park.

Yr Elen from the approach to Carnedd Uchaf

2. *The round of Cwm Caseg & Cwm Llafar*

Outline: *A long, elevated walk by a broad grass ridge into the heart of the Carneddau with spectacular views in clear conditions. This is followed by an undulating walk across the stoney plateau to Carnedd Llewelyn and Carnedd Dafydd with a long descent into Cwm Llafar.*

Distance: *17km/10½ miles.*

Height gained: *1,120m/3,684ft.*

Summits: *Carnedd Uchaf, Foel Grach, Carnedd Llewelyn & Carnedd Dafydd (Yr Elen optional).*

Starting point: *Gerlan in upper Bethesda (grid ref: SH 633 663). There is very limited parking in Gerlan, but official parking is available off the high street (A5) in Bethesda, with a walk up to Gerlan to start. Grid ref: SH 623 667.*

THE MAIN BACKBONE OF THE HIGH CARNEDDAU lies remote from any approach requiring a long walk in. This route uses a long, easy-angled ridge to turn the 5km/3 mile approach into a gentle ascent. The ridge ends on the northern edge of the high Carneddau plateau from where you can tick off most of the highest summits with minimal effort.

The route: From Gerlan turn left into 'Ciltwllan', a narrow lane which eventually becomes unsurfaced beyond the final houses and cottages at Ciltwllan. Continue along this track to its end beside sheep pens and the remains of an old brick pumping station. Turn right onto a path which runs beside the stone wall, then, almost immediately, bear diagonally-left on a faint path past a huge rounded boulder up towards a stile on the skyline.

Stiles take you out of the final fields and onto the open hillside of Gyrn Wigau. With this minor top behind you the angle eases and you meet a Landrover track in the approach to Drosgl. The path to the right here contours around the hillside avoiding the climb to both Drosgl

and Bera Bach. If you would rather take in these summits follow the track ahead.

For the easiest option bear right on the contouring path which becomes more vague in the approach to Carnedd Uchaf. Alternatively, head for the castellated sub top of Yr Aryg and then Carnedd Uchaf. In poor visibility you will need to walk on a compass bearing and it is not always easy to decide when you are on the summit. If you have a GPS unit this is the place to use it.

From Carnedd Uchaf the main Carnedd 'highway' heads almost due south to Foel Grach, then south-southwest to Carnedd Llewelyn, the highest summit in the range. Again, in poor visibility it is not easy to determine which of the many cairns marks the highest point. The summit has a ruined circular stone cairn which gives some shelter from the wind.

(To include Yr Elen—a 2.5km/1½ mile out-and-back walk—head west to join the short narrow connecting ridge. You will need to return the same way to continue, but a contouring path can be used to avoid

Looking down Carnedd Dafydd's northwest ridge towards Bethesda

Crossing 'The Saddle', between Carnedd Llewelyn and Carnedd Dafydd

the climb back to Carnedd Llewelyn. This breaks away right soon after the narrow ridge merges into the final slopes of the mountain.)

From Carnedd Llewelyn follow the main path south over Bwlch Cyfryw-drum ('*The Saddle*') then follow the broad ridge as it swings west along the rim of the precipice known as Ysgolion Duon—the 'Black Ladders'—to Carnedd Dafydd. This is a lovely walk, easy-angled, elevated and with wide views on both sides—left to the rock wedge of Tryfan and the northern cwms of the Glyderau and right into the gulf of Cwm Llafar.

From Carnedd Dafydd descend northwest close to the edge of the northern cliffs. The upper section is rather indistinct over scree and boulders and would be difficult in poor visibility (beware of false trails leading right towards the complex northern cliffs of the mountain). Lower down where the angles eases the ridge becomes easier to follow. Continue down the now grassy ridge to join the path beside Afon Llafar. Turn left and follow this path back to the lane end beside a small waterworks building. Follow the lane right, back to Gerlan and Bethesda.

Carnedd Dafydd and the prominent nose of the Llech Ddu Spur

3. Cwm Llafar Horseshoe

Outline: SCRAMBLE *A long but gentle walk into a spectacular mountain cwm is follow by easy scrambling with a little exposure on a fine shattered arête in a superb setting. Once on the high plateau, easy walking around the rim of Cwm Llafar above the impressive Black Ladders leads to Carnedd Llewelyn and Yr Elen. Descent is by the rocky northeast ridge of Yr Elen into Cwm Caseg.*

Distance: *17km/10½ miles.*

Height gained: *1,200/3,900ft.*

Summits: *Carnedd Dafydd, Carnedd Llewelyn & Yr Elen.*

Starting point: *Gerlan in upper Bethesda (Grid ref: SH 633 663). There is very limited parking in Gerlan, but official parking is available off the high street (A5) in Bethesda, with a walk up to Gerlan to start. Grid ref: SH 623 667.*

THE DARK DRIPPING PRECIPICE known as the 'Black Ladders' (Ysgolion Duon) has a fearsome reputation for its hard, exposed winter climbs, but yields few quality rock climbs due to the amount of drainage taken by the face. This produces wet slimy rock and accounts for the dark black colour from which the precipice takes its name. The main face is a spectacular near vertical wall some 300 metres high and almost 1km/¾ mile wide. Only at its western edge is there any suitable weakness to tempt the scrambler were a shattered nose-like arête (Llech Ddu Spur) protrudes from the main face. The lower section of the ridge is definitely off-limits to the scrambler, but a detour into the cwm to the right allows access to the middle and upper sections of the ridge which provide the best scrambling.

The Llech Ddu Spur is a superb route onto the high tops of the Carneddau and sadly almost the only scramble of its kind in the entire group. It is of a similar standard to the North Ridge of Tryfan or the rock ridge of Y Gribin. By the described route the scrambling is straightforward and there is surprisingly little exposure, although care in finding the correct route is required. It is not recommended in

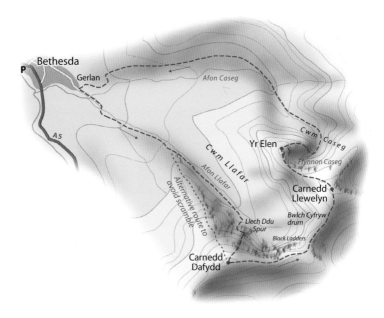

Yr Elen and the northeast ridge seen from the slopes of Carnedd Llewelyn

poor visibility or under winter conditions. *(The scramble section of the route can be avoided by ascending the northwest ridge of Carnedd Dafydd—see opposite.)*

The route: From Gerlan continue along the gently rising lane for almost 1km/¾ mile. Immediately after the road curves right over the river for the second time, bear left along a 'Private Road'. In a few yards and before the waterworks, bear right over a stile beside a gate. Go ahead up the field edge to a ladder stile in the top left corner. Turn left over the stile then right onto a path which shortly passes to the right of ruins. The path is well defined now and soon you are walking with the shapely cone of Yr Elen ahead. Immediately after a footbridge the path forks—keep right as signed and soon cross a wall by means of a ladder stile.

Keep ahead aiming approximately for the gap between Carnedd Dafydd and Yr Elen through a large field to the final stile before the open mountain pastures. The path is better defined now and in about

200m, just before a small square enclosure with iron railings, splits. *(To avoid the Llech Ddu Spur scramble, bear right up Carnedd Dafydd's northwest ridge at this point.)* Keep ahead on the well-defined footpath parallel to Afon Llafar and walk almost to the head of the cwm below the towering cliffs of the 'Black Ladders'.

To the right of the main cliff there is a large triangular buttress which forms the base of the Llech Ddu Spur. This is a classic example of a 'truncated spur', created by a glacier cutting off a ridge or spur which would previously have protruded into the valley. For the scrambler a direct line is impossible, but a detour to the right allows access to the upper ridge which gives pleasant scrambling onto the summit slopes of Carnedd Dafydd.

Head towards the right-hand end of the triangular buttress where a black stain from a small cascade can be seen. Immediately to the left of the cascade a narrow path zig-zags steeply up scree into the cwm above. Continue steeply and directly up to a point almost level with the base of the large crag to the right which is split by a prominent gully or chimney. The faint path now turns left across a shattered grassy terrace to a small grass platform on the skyline by white quartz rocks. This is the start of the scrambling.

Scramble up the broken wall directly above. The exact line can be varied at will but remains at a similar standard. Higher up, the ridge levels and a short easy section with small pinnacles follows.

One of the pinnacles on the Llech Du Spur with Yr Elen behind

The angle steepens again and pleasant, easy scrambling with little exposure continues until the ridge eventually merges into the upper shattered slopes of the mountain. Continue up to arrive on the ridge a little to the east of the summit.

From Carnedd Dafydd head east along the broad, easy, almost level ridge with superb views right into the northern cwms of the Glyderau and left into the gulf of Cwm Llafar where you will get good views back to the Llech Ddu Spur. The ridge soon swings north over Bwlch Cyfryw-drum where a short rise leads to the highest summit in the range—Carnedd Llewelyn—just 21m lower than Snowdon.

From Carnedd Llewelyn take the path which heads out west across the plateau. Soon you have a view of Yr Elen's impressive northeast face rising above the hidden Cwm Caseg. The connecting ridge looks quite striking too but sadly provides little scrambling.

From Yr Elen the most interesting descent is by the northeast ridge which falls directly from the summit—a mixture of shattered spiky rocks separated by grass. The main interest is in the upper section where you will need your hands here and there. Once the scree to your right is replaced by grass, break away from the crest and descend to the tiny lake—Ffynnon Caseg—visible below in its remote hidden cwm.

From the outflow of the lake descend just to the right of the stream, gradually moving further to the right to avoid boggy ground as you descend. As the valley flattens a path establishes itself at the point where the drier slopes to the right meet the boggy, waterlogged ground of the valley base. Where the valley opens out, follow the narrow but visible path which takes a contouring line above the waterlogged valley floor ahead, following the line of a now dried out but still visible leat.

Follow the path for about 1.5km/1 mile before looking for a faint path which drops diagonally-left to a group of well-built sheep pens which can be seen below. Join a farm track by the sheep pens and follow this for another 2km/1¼ miles until you reach a small building on the left. Turn left here down a wall-enclosed track which leads into a lane by cottages. Follow the lane back to Gerlan.

Graig yr Ysfa from upper Cwm Eigiau

4. *The Carneddau from the east via Cwm Eigiau*

Outline: *A long, secluded valley approach to an impressive lonely cwm is followed by an improbable but surprisingly easy scramble up the massive headwall to Carnedd Llewelyn's east ridge. Easy walking up the broad ridge to the summit, then north to the adjacent summit of Foel Grach. Descent is by grassy, trackless ground to the twin lakes of Melynllyn and Dulyn and then by rough Landrover tracks to complete the round.*

Distance: *15.5km/9½ miles.*

Height gained: *914m/3,000ft.*

Summits: *Carnedd Llewelyn & Foel Grach.*

Starting point: *There is free parking for several cars at the end of the old lane which rises from Tal-y-Bont on the B5106, 2km/1¼ miles north of Dolgarrog. Grid ref. SH 732 663.*

FROM THE EAST, the Carneddau is at its most inaccessible—long, remote hanging valleys snake down from the high tops requiring long approach walks well before any climbing begins. Cwm Eigiau is the longest and most dramatic of these and were it not for the narrow lane which climbs steeply from the Conwy Valley to the mouth of the cwm, any approach from this side would be out of the question for the normal walker.

The valley is silent and neglected now but reminders of a time not too long ago when there was quarrying, dam building and mining in the valley are much in evidence.

The low-grade scramble from the valley head to the ridge at Bwlch Eryl Farchog is straightforward, but not recommended in poor visibility or wintery conditions when the correct route could be hard to follow making the ascent potentially hazardous.

The route: From the parking area continue along the track which heads directly up the valley towards the dark crags of Craig Eigiau and the sweeping cone of Pen Llithrig y Wrach.

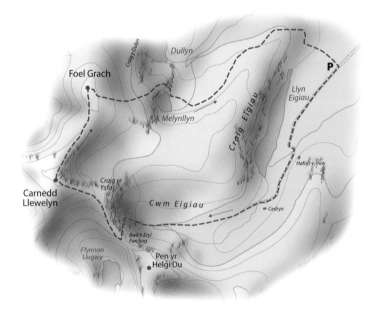

At the dam follow the track as it swings left over the river, then right to continue up the valley. Ignore forks on the left to the dwelling of 'Hafod-y-rhiw' and a little further on to the empty 'Cedryn'. Shortly, the track crosses the river again and begins a gradual climb passing a small cottage on the right (the last habitable building of the valley).

If you have studied your map, anticipation builds here as you wait for the view up to the massive headwall of Craig yr Ysfa, one of the favoured crags of the pioneer rock climbers. Its twin buttresses are separated by a great scree filled gully known as 'The Amphitheatre'. The ridge which rises from this scree is known as Amphitheatre Buttress and provides an easy rock climb of over 300m. It was first climbed by the Keswick duo known as the Abraham Brothers in the early 1900s.

This cwm is a wonderfully remote spot but it is not unspoiled. The track ends at ruined buildings associated with the nearby quarry workings which recall a time not too long ago when this silent spot would have been busy with the noise and activity of mining.

This is a good place to take stock of the route ahead. Craig yr Ysfa is composed of two huge buttresses separated by a deep gully with a large triangular scree cone at its base. This apparently impregnable headwall has a surprisingly easy escape route although it is not recommended in poor visibility or wintery conditions. From the lowest rocks of the left-hand buttress a narrow footpath slants leftwards up the scree to a point where a heathery rib on the left meets the clean rocks to the right. From here simple scrambling by the easiest line leads up past a solitary sapling onto the lowest point of the ridge above (Bwlch Eryl Farchog). This is a route used by rock climbers coming over from Cwm Llugwy to reach the foot of Craig yr Ysfa.

From the ruins veer left to cross the river by a raised dyke and walk up towards a small quarry, then bear right below spoil heaps to pick up a path which traverses off towards the crag. This is faint but visible and runs parallel to the stream on the right keeping above the often marshy ground on both sides.

At the base of the scree the path ascends directly to the lowest rocks of the left-hand buttress, then swings left along the base of the crag, still rising steeply. At the top of the scree the rocks on the right

The upper section of Carnedd Llewelyn's east ridge under winter conditions

meet with the vegetated heathery ribs on the left. The path is visible as it crosses easy rocks then heather to a prominent grass and scree gully with a sapling above. Ascend the gully passing the tree to a point where a prominent footpath forks left, then up. Follow this footpath steeply up to the skyline.

By the correct (and easiest) line this scramble is straightforward, but things become much harder and exposed if you traverse too far left.

From the bwlch go right along the ridge where simple scrambling over a short rock step leads onto the broad east ridge of the mountain. Take care near the rim of 'The Amphitheatre'—a drop of several hundred metres—where you will get stunning views back down to the ruined quarry buildings visited earlier framed by the gully sides.

The ridge leads uneventfully to the summit where a small drystone shelter marks the highest point.

From Carnedd Llewelyn follow the main ridge northeast, then due north to Foel Grach, 1.5km/1 mile distant. If you have any doubts about the location of Foel Grach look for the little refuge hut a few metres below the summit rocks on the east side.

(Warning—In good visibility the descent to Melynllyn is both easy and straightforward. In poor visibility however, it would be difficult to locate the grassy tongue separating the two lakes without a compass or GPS unit and there are cliffs above each lake.)

From Foel Grach head southeast, initially across the broad grass plateau (no path) aiming just to the left of the distant Pen Llithrig y Wrach, then veer more to the left in the direction of Creigiau Gleision's left-hand crags. Keep on this course until you reach a conspicuous area of bouldery rocks (rather than just grass). At this point turn left and head directly down hill with the broad lower valley ahead (slightly north of due east).

Lower down, the two lakes (one on either side) will come into view. Continue down the grass ridge bearing right lower down to join an access track by the outflow of Melynllyn. Follow this track back to the parking area (about 4km/2½ miles).

As you head down the track there are good views back to the dark cwm containing Dulyn (black lake) with its dramatic headwall and the higher but brighter and far less foreboding Melynllyn (yellow lake).

Looking back up lonely Cwm Eigiau near the end of the walk

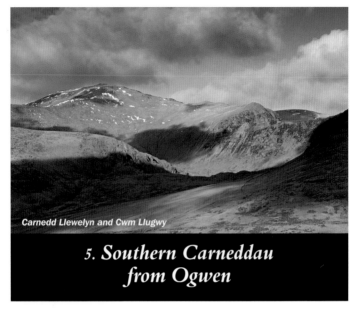

Carnedd Llewelyn and Cwm Llugwy

5. *Southern Carneddau from Ogwen*

Outline: *A steady ascent and a short easy, scramble to Pen-yr Ole Wen is followed by an elevated ridge walk over three high summits with wide views south to the Glyderau and Tryfan. Descent is by Carnedd Llewelyn's long southeast ridge, across the narrow Bwlch Eryl Farchog to Pen yr Helgi Du and then by the gentle ridge of Y Braich.*

Distance: *19km/11¾ miles.*

Height gained: *1,400m/4,410ft.*

Summits: *Pen-yr Ole Wen, Carnedd Dafydd, Carnedd Llewelyn, Yr Elen & Pen yr Helgi Du.*

Starting point: *There is ample free parking at the eastern end of Llyn Ogwen between Glan Dena and Gwern Gof Uchaf. Grid ref: SH 668 606.*

THE MOST POPULAR ACCESS TO THE HIGH TOPS of the Carneddau is from the Ogwen valley to the south which avoids the long approach walks required from the north, east and west. This route is excellent in either a clockwise or anticlockwise direction and once the climbing is done, you can cruise along the fine, elevated ridge between Carnedd Dafydd and Carnedd Llewelyn with minimal effort. Views are superb, particularly south to Tryfan, the Glyderau and Cwm Idwal.

If you need to shorten the walk, this can be done at Bwlch Eryl Farchog by taking the path down to Ffynnon Llugwy and then following the reservoir access road down to the A5. You can also leave out the extension to Yr Elen.

The route: From the A5, cross the bridge and follow the track past the house 'Glan Dena', situated in a small conifer wood at the eastern end of Llyn Ogwen. Continue along the track towards 'Tal y Llyn Ogwen'

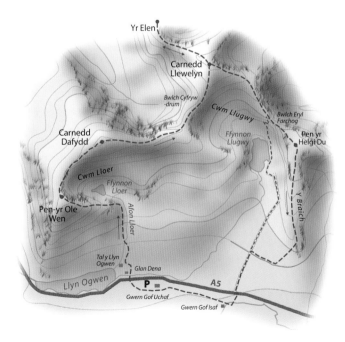

Looking back to Pen yr Ole Wen from Pen-yr Helgi Du

farm, but turn right up to a stile in the wall immediately before the farm. After the stile, the path curves right to follow Afon Lloer. Cross the stream higher up and follow it until the angle eases as you approach Cwm Lloer.

Head left before you reach the lake to begin the ascent of Pen-yr Ole Wen's east ridge. A broken rock spur is negotiated by a short easy gully scramble to gain a well-defined path which keeps close to the crags overlooking the south wall of the Cwm Lloer to the right.

Pen-yr Ole Wen is the perfect viewpoint for the magnificent hollow of Cwm Idwal, enclosed by Glyder Fawr and Y Garn and is well worth the short detour to the top of the southwest ridge.

From Pen-yr Ole Wen a good path heads northeast along the ridge to Carnedd Dafydd (about 1.5km/1 mile away). From Carnedd Dafydd the path continues along the broad ridge above the huge cliffs known as the 'Black Ladders' (Ysgolion Duon). A short drop to Bwlch Cyfryw-drum is followed by a steady ascent over scree to Carnedd Llewelyn, Snowdonia's third highest mountain and the highest point in the Carneddau.

If you want to include the summit of Yr Elen it is a straightforward 3km/2 mile out-and-back detour along the northwest ridge.

From Carnedd Llewelyn follow the broad east ridge with the deep glacial trough of Cwm Eigiau ahead. The ridge is steep at first, then more gentle and grassy until you reach the rim of Craig yr Ysfa and its famous 'Amphitheatre'. The ridge narrows now and there is a little scrambling to reach Bwlch Eryl Farchog. *(You could shorten the walk here if needed by taking the path which zig-zags down to the lake and following the reservoir road down to the A5.)* A short scramble from the bwlch leads to Pen yr Helgi Du, another superb viewpoint, particularly for Tryfan seen dramatically across the valley.

From here, head due south along the gentle, rounded ridge of Y Braich. Almost at the bottom of the ridge pass through a gap in a crossing wall and bear right over open ground to cross a leat by a footbridge. This feeds water into the nearby Llyn Cowlyd Reservoir. Turn right now and follow the leat to the reservoir access road leading to up Ffynnon Llugwy. Turn left down the road to the A5.

To avoid the 2km/1¼ miles or so back along the A5, turn left along the road and just before a small conifer wood, go right over the stile and make your way through a boulder-strewn field to a group of old pines. The stile here leads onto a bridleway, once the main road through the valley. Turn right and follow the path back past Gwern Gof Uchaf farm to reach the A5.

Looking along the Black Ladders

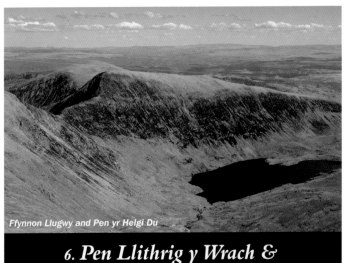

Ffynnon Llugwy and Pen yr Helgi Du

6. Pen Llithrig y Wrach & Pen yr Helgi Du from Capel Curig

Outline: *A gentle walk over boggy moors from the A5 and a short steep ascent lead to the excellent viewpoint of Pen Llithrig y Wrach. This is followed by a walk along the connecting ridge to Pen yr Helgi Du and a gentle descent of Y Braich with stunning views of Tryfan. Easy, level walking back to Capel Curig.*

Distance: *14km/8¾ miles.*

Height gained: *854m/2,800ft.*

Summits: *Pen Llithrig y Wrach & Pen yr Helgi Du.*

Starting point: *Begin the walk from the car park situated behind the shops in Capel Curig. Grid ref: SH 721 582*

THESE TWO SHAPELY HILLS ARE OFTEN IGNORED or overlooked in favour of their higher neighbours, but they are major summits, not foothills and if they stood elsewhere they would be recognised as such. This route links both summits by a fine grassy ridge and offers stunning views of Tryfan in the descent of Y Braich.

The route: Turn left out of the car park and walk over the old bridge to join the main road with the shops to your left. Turn left and walk along the A5 for about 1km/¾ mile.

About 100m beyond a house on the right ('Bryn Heulog') turn right onto a signed footpath. Walk diagonally-left up the gentle hillside, initially following a line of power cables, before they veer away to the left. Quite soon the buttresses of Tryfan's East Face come into view over the rounded shoulder of Gallt yr Ogof to the left.

Pass a stone-built farm on the left and continue ahead to a ladder stile beside an old iron gate. Bear right after the stile and follow the well worn footpath over the open moors with the cone of Pen Llithrig y Wrach directly ahead and widening views of the Ogwen valley to the left. The path is well used and easy enough to follow (although often wet).

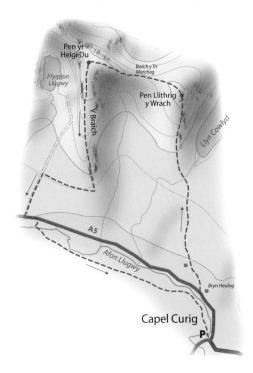

Higher up the path crosses a footbridge over one of the leats which channel water from the southern slopes of the Carneddau into the Llyn Cowlyd Reservoir. Follow the path half-left after the footbridge to cross a second footbridge over the leat again. The good path to the right here leads along the shore of Llyn Cowlyd. Ignore this path taking a less well-used line straight ahead up the mountain's broad south ridge. Higher up the path zig-zags steeply through rocks and heather to the summit.

Pen Llithrig y Wrach (a curious name meaning 'head of the slippery slope of the witch') is a superb viewpoint for the southern Carneddau and the rocky summits of the Glyderau seen across the valley.

To continue, follow the mountain's gentle west ridge over Bwlch y Tri Marchog (another curious name meaning 'pass of the three horsemen') to the summit of Pen yr Helgi Du, an equally good viewpoint for the eastern Carneddau and southwest across the Ogwen valley to Tryfan and the Glyderau.

From here turn due south (left) and walk down the broad ridge of Y Braich to the stile which leads onto the leat at the foot of the ridge. Cross the bridge here and turn right beside the leat. At the road which leads up to the reservoir of Ffynnon Llugwy, turn left and walk down to the A5.

Turn left along the road for about 250m, then cross over and climb the ladder stile directly opposite. Take the obvious path ahead through a boulder-strewn field towards a group of Scots pines. A ladder stile leads onto a bridleway here which is all that now remains of the old road through the Ogwen valley, built by Lord Penrhyn in 1800. Turn left and follow the bridleway back to Capel Curig (about 3km/2 miles).

Looking west to Tryfan from Creigiau Gleision

7. Greigiau Gleision & the Crafnant Skyline

Outline: *This route follows the skyline above the Crafnant valley giving superb views west towards the Glyderau, Ogwen and Snowdon, as well as to Crafnant itself. The featureless approach to Greigiau Gleision will require careful route finding.*

Distance: *12.5km/7½ miles.*

Height gained: *790m/2,580ft.*

Summits: *Creigiau Gleision.*

Starting point: *Llyn Crafnant Forest Enterprises car park just before the lake. WC facilities are provided and a parking fee is required. Grid ref. SH 755 618.*

THIS SOUTHEASTERN SPUR OF THE CARNEDDAU provides quite a contrast to the higher tops—gentle rolling fells enclosing lush wooded valleys and intimate lakes. The walking here reflects this pastoral, rather than high mountain landscape.

The route: Turn left out of the car park and walk down the lane crossing over the bridge. In about 700m (almost ½ mile), bear left up a rising lane opposite a stone cottage on the right. Follow the lane round a sharp left-hand bend and pass a house up on the right. The lane now becomes an unsurfaced track which should be followed through a sharp right, then sharp left-hand bend. At the next bend keep right ignoring the track to the left which leads to a gate with a farm beyond. Zig-zag up to a ladder stile in the fence. Go over the stile and keep ahead on a narrow, faint but visible path (marked here and there by low marker posts). Take a more or less direct line up the hillside if you lose the path, until you reach a contouring farm track. Turn left along the track and shortly, at a fork, bear right.

In clear conditions views open out to the head of the valley where you should just be able to see Llyn Crafnant. Moel Siabod is the commanding peak ahead.

En-route from Creigiau Gleision to Crimpiau

Follow the grass track/path to a gate and ladder stile over the wall leading onto the upper moors. Follow the sunken path which heads across the moors towards the knobbly crags of Creigiau Gleision. Keep to the most obvious path which eventually leads to a junction of wire fences and a ladder stile. Go over the stile and keep to the obvious path which soon bears left as the higher tops of the Carneddau come into view. Shortly, turn left over a stile in the fence and follow the good path which heads half-right through the heather.

Soon conifers come into view ahead and the path bends right to a level marshy area. Cross this and make your way through the heather to the fence beyond. Turn left and follow a faint footpath beside the fence or cross the fence and follow the better path on the far side. The fence soon turns right and rises more steeply and the path (on the right side of the fence) becomes much better defined. At the top of the rise cross the fence on the left in the corner and follow the obvious footpath which veers leftwards along the rounded knobbly ridge.

At the first summit you are greeted in clear conditions by a breathtaking view down to Llyn Cowlyd and across to Pen Llithrig y

Wrach, its southern slopes plunging almost 300m to the shore of the lake and ahead between the hills to Tryfan, the Glyderau and Snowdon.

Continue along the ridge rising and falling over rocky summits to the main top.

Make a short steep descent from the summit (to the south) to a flat grassy area followed by a slight rise to the first of many small rocky tops. From here walk along the flat rounded ridge to the next top, then drop more steeply to a small flat area or bwlch. The path keeps to the right of the next rocky top (Moel Ddefaid) followed by another steep descent to a large flat marshy area occupying the next bwlch.

Keep to the right of the marshy area and the large rocky summit which follows (Craig Wen). Walk over the shoulder of Craig Wen and descend to stone walls. Go through a gap in the first wall, then half-right through a second gap and follow the path down to the next bwlch.

Take the path ahead which bears half-right at first, then curves leftwards to rise more directly to the summit of Crimpiau.

The wide mountain panoramas which you have enjoyed to the west are now complemented by a dramatic view down into the Crafnant valley. From here almost the whole route is visible including the next stage of the walk down into the valley and along the left-hand side of the lake.

From Crimpiau the path heads east to join the Capel Curig/Llyn Crafnant path almost at its highest point. Turn left along this path keeping left at a fork almost immediately. Follow the obvious path down into the valley to a stile beside a gateway in a wall. Go left through the gateway, then bear half-right through a small open field to join a lane by a gate. Take the second left here (first left leads to 'Blaen-y-Nant' farm) passing two chalets on the left. Follow the lane over the stream and immediately before the gate to 'Hendre Bach' turn right over a footbridge and follow the footpath left around the house and through an area of young pines to join a broader path at the top of the bank. Turn right and follow the path/forest road close to the lake. At the end of the lake turn left down the lane to return to the forest car park.

The West Face of Tryfan from the head of Nant Ffrancon

The Glyderau

Looking into the northern cwms of Glyder Fach and Glyder Fawr from Pen-yr Ole Wen

The Glyderau

THE GLYDERAU FORM A HIGH CURVING RIDGE bounded to the north and east by Nant Ffrancon and the Ogwen valley, and to the south and west by Dyffryn Mymbyr and the Llanberis Pass. At its eastern extremity lies the village of Capel Curig; at its northwestern end the town of Bethesda. All the high summits lie along this main watershed which reaches its apex in the high 'other worldly' plateau of Glyder Fawr and Glyder Fach—a quiver of rock spikes and shattered slabs. The exceptions are Elidir Fawr, famous for its quarry-scarred western slopes which rise above Llanberis, and the startling rock tower of Tryfan, which has delighted travellers on the A5 for centuries. Both these peaks lie on off-shoot spurs at either end of the main ridge.

Sandwiched between the Carneddau and Snowdon, the Glyderau could be said to be a good mix of the two—or maybe a transition. Like Snowdon there are fine rocky ridges, dramatic glacial cwms and sparkling mountain lakes, and there is also a wealth of rock scenery,

but the main summits of the group are flat and bulky like the Carneddau and—with the exception of Tryfan—lack Snowdon's narrow graceful crests.

After Snowdon, these are the most popular and most frequented summits in Snowdonia and contain some of its most famous sights. Top of the list has to be Tryfan. Who can forget their first glimpse of its towering east face sliding into view from behind the rounded shoulders of Gallt yr Ogof. And Tryfan delivers all it promises—the scramble up the famous North Ridge to the airy summit is every bit as good as it looks—a true rock peak.

Close by is Bristly Ridge, often used as a scrambling link between Tryfan and Glyder Fach. Here the rock theme is continued with 'The Cantilever'—a huge table of rock near the summit which has been famous since the eighteenth century travels of Thomas Pennant. The illustrations of Pennant standing on the table are little different from the photographs taken by today's visitors. Castell y Gwynt ('Castle of the Winds'), a jumble of rock spikes on the broad ridge between Glyder

Fach and Glyder Fawr has likewise been photographed and painted for centuries and provides one of the finest foregrounds for views of Snowdon.

In the heart of the group is Cwm Idwal; a great rock amphitheatre cradling the famous Llyn Idwal and overlooked by the dripping cleft of Twll Du, better known as 'The Devil's Kitchen'. Llyn Idwal is probably the most famous mountain lake in Snowdonia and has been written about, photographed and painted for centuries. It also has the distinction of being the location where it was first realised that the mountains of Britain had been glaciated in the distant past.

The range has two very different faces—one dramatic, the other undulating and almost featureless. The northern and eastern faces have been carved into an assortment of crag-lined cwms, cliffs and sharp arêtes, whilst the southern and western slopes are rounded and lacking in architectural complexity.

Cwm Idwal and The Devil's Kitchen from the shores of Llyn Idwal

Y Garn and Foel Goch from Llyn Ogwen

The main routes of ascent reflect this stark contrast. Llyn Ogwen—situated in the centre of the group—is the main base, giving access to the most popular summits from the western end of the lake. Y Garn, the Devil's Kitchen, Bristly Ridge, the Gribin Ridge, Cwm Bochlwyd and Tryfan are all accessible from here, whilst the more demanding routes on Tryfan's eastern flanks are more conveniently accessed from the eastern end of Llyn Ogwen.

From the south, access is limited, not because of difficulty but apparent lack of interest. But all is not lost; the single route of note from this side has one highlight, a beautiful lake—Llyn Cwmffynnon—which lies hidden in a hollow above the famous Pen-y-Gwryd Hotel, providing a foreground for one of the finest views of Crib Goch and Crib y Ddysgl.

The northern end of the group is most dramatically viewed from Nant Ffrancon, but access is difficult from here and there are few recognised paths. Access is easier from the west, where long ridge walks taking in nearly all the northern tops, can be started and finished at Nant Peris where there is ample parking.

The west face of Tryfan from Cwm Idwal

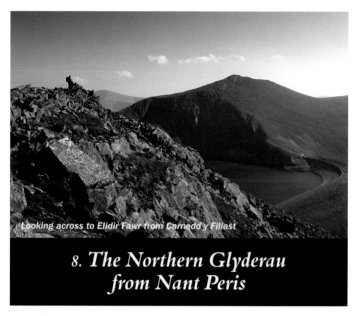

Looking across to Elidir Fawr from Carnedd y Filiast

8. The Northern Glyderau from Nant Peris

Outline: *A moderate approach to gain an elevated grass rib with wide views. Once on the main Glyder ridge, most of the northern summits can be accessed with minimal effort. Descent is by the dramatic Cwm Dudodyn.*

Distance: *14.25km/8¾ miles.*

Height gained: *1,033m/3,400ft.*

Summits: *Mynydd Perfedd, Carnedd y Filiast & Elidir Fawr.*

Starting point: *There is a large car park and WC facilities in Nant Peris. Grid ref: SH 606 583.*

THE NORTHERN TOPS OF THE GLYDER RANGE have one big disadvantage over their better known southerly neighbours—poor access. The attractive eastern cwms and spurs which rise above Nant Ffrancon are steep, pathless and difficult to negotiate, whilst the northern and western slopes have been ruined beyond repair by quarrying. Only to the southwest is there any suitable access.

This route uses the excellent and little used Esgair Dudodyn ridge as an approach to Bwlch y Brecan from where all the northern summits can be reached. Unfortunately they are not strung together on one tidy ridge, so some retracing of steps is unavoidable.

The route: From the car park turn left along the road passing the 'Vaynol Arms' and immediately before a chapel turn right down a narrow lane. Take the first left before the stream and follow the rising lane to a stone cottage on the right. Ignore the sharp turning to the right, staying on the lane and going through the gateway ahead. Immediately before the next gateway, turn right through a small gate and walk up beside the wall to a stile in the top wall. Continue up to a second stile over the wall.

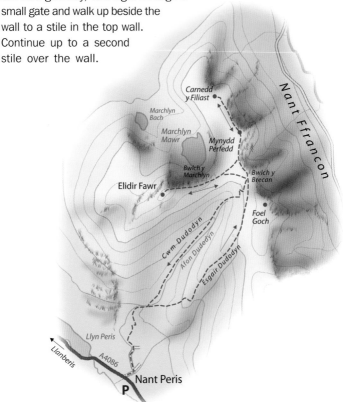

The path is now better defined and after running beside the wall for a few metres bears half-right and then zig-zags up the field.

Soon the path curves right to run beside the tumbling stream. Pass a footbridge on the left and go through the gateway in the wall ahead. In about 75m, bear half-right onto a faint footpath which heads towards the base of the ridge ahead. At a wall bear left beside it to make a short steep climb onto the ridge. With most of the hard work done you can now enjoy an easy elevated jaunt with views across Cwm Dudodyn towards Elidir Fawr.

Where the ridge merges into the broad mountainside of Foel Goch, take the contouring path which veers to the left to Bwlch y Brecan. *(From here you can make a short detour south—up to the right—to Foel Goch, but a return to the bwlch is needed to continue.)* Rise from here to Mynydd Perfedd rather than following the contouring footpath left. Carnedd y Filiast is an easy almost level 1km/¾ mile stroll across the plateau. Take care in poor visibility as you approach the latter summit. Huge slabs tumble into Cwm Graianog just a few metres from the stile over the wall!

Return to Mynydd Perfedd and follow the ridge southwest to Bwlch y Marchlyn, then continue up to the shattered summit of Elidir Fawr. To return to Nant Peris, a path which drops steeply southwest, gives a quick descent but it is knee shatteringly steep. A more pleasant option is to return to Bwlch y Marchlyn and take the contouring path to Bwlch y Brecan, then descend the grass slope at the head of Cwm Dudodyn to pick up the path on the true right bank of Afon Dudodyn. Cross the footbridge passed earlier and retrace the outward journey.

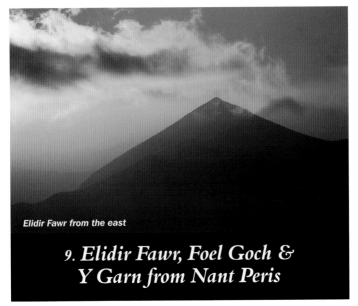

Elidir Fawr from the east

9. *Elidir Fawr, Foel Goch &*
Y Garn from Nant Peris

Outline: *A tough, steep approach to Elidir Fawr is followed by undulating ridge walking to Y Garn. A gentle descent to Llyn y Cŵn above the Devil's Kitchen and an attractive descent beside the tumbling Afon Las.*

Distance: *13km/8 miles.*

Height gained: *1,230m/4,000ft.*

Summits: *Elidir Fawr, Foel Goch & Y Garn.*

Starting point: *There is a large car park and WC facilities in Nant Peris. Grid ref: SH 606 583.*

THIS IS A MUCH TOUGHER OPTION than the previous route and can be extended to include the outliers of Mynydd Perfedd and Carnedd y Ffiliast if you are feeling particularly energetic.

The route: From the car park turn left along the road passing the 'Vaynol Arms' and immediately before a chapel, turn right down a narrow lane. Take the first left before the stream and follow the rising lane to a stone

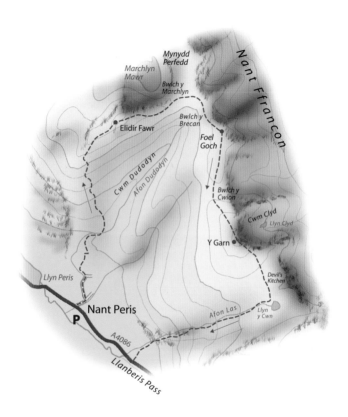

cottage on the right. Ignore the sharp turning to the right, staying on the lane and going through the gateway ahead. Immediately before the next gateway, turn right through a small gate and walk up beside the wall to a stile in the top wall. Continue up to a second stile over the wall. The path is now better defined and after running beside the wall for a few metres bears half-right and then zig-zags up the field.

Soon the path curves right to run beside the tumbling stream. Follow the path to a footbridge and cross over. The hard work now begins. A grass path rises directly up from here to a ladder stile onto the upper, open slopes of the mountain. Continue the ascent on the same direct line and you will arrive at the summit. It is possible to ease the steep ascent a little by taking a diagonal line to the left to join the southwest ridge and follow this to the summit, but any ascent of the mountain from this side is steep and the direct line gets it over with quickest.

Standing separate from the main Glyder ridge, Elidir Fawr is an excellent viewpoint, particularly for Snowdon which rises dramatically across the valley beyond Nant Peris.

From Elidir Fawr the ridge descends initially northeast, then east to Bwlch y Marchlyn. *(If you intend to include the outliers of Mynydd Perfeddd and Carnedd y Filiast follow the rounded ridge northeast from here to Mynydd Perfedd, then north to Carnedd y Filiast. Return over Mynydd Perfedd to Bwlch y Brecan to continue.)* A contouring path leads effortlessly from Bwlch y Marchlyn to Bwlch y Brecan, separating Mynydd Perfedd from Foel Goch. For Foel Goch a short, steep ascent (about 120m) brings you to the summit with its stunning views into Nant Ffrancon. Head south from here down the rounded ridge past Bwlch y Cywion to the saddle beyond. The ridge rises again to Y Garn, another fine viewpoint, particularly down the northeast ridge to Llyn Ogwen with Tryfan beyond.

Follow the rim of Cwm Clyd southeast for about 500m before turning south with the path for a gentle stoney descent to Llyn y Cŵn, perched in a hollow on the watershed of the broad flat ridge separating Nant Peris from Cwm Idwal. To the left the dark cleft of the Devil's Kitchen remains out of sight but is worth the short detour for the view of Llyn Idwal framed by the walls of the gorge.

From the northern edge of Llyn y Cŵn the Nant Peris path descends southwest steepening as it runs beside Afon Las. Lower down a ladder stile takes you off the open mountain to weave between small crags and stunted trees. Pass a cottage on the left where a stile leads over the wall and walk down the access track to the road. Turn right along the road to return to the car park at Nant Peris (about 1km/¾ mile).

Y Garn, the 'Armchair Mountain', from Llyn Ogwen

10. Glyder Fawr & Y Garn by Y Gribin

Outline: SCRAMBLE *An easy walk to a high mountain cwm and sheltered lake followed by low-grade straightforward scrambling up a rocky ridge onto the high Glyder ridge. A rocky descent followed by a more gradual climb takes you to the summit of Y Garn. Descent is by Y Garn's steep northeast ridge.*

Distance: *11km/6¾ miles.*

Height gained: *1,080m/3,530ft.*

Summits: *Glyder Fawr & Y Garn.*

Starting point: *Parking is available at the western end of Llyn Ogwen and in lay-bys along the lake. Start the walk from the refreshment kiosk. Grid ref: SH 649 604.*

SOMETIMES REFERRED TO AS THE 'ARMCHAIR MOUNTAIN', from the two enclosing ridges which embrace the tiny Llyn Clyd, Y Garn dominates the view westwards along Llyn Ogwen. Almost invisible from Ogwen, Glyder Fawr's moment of glory comes as you head south along the

A5 through Nant Ffrancon where it heads a complex of huge slabs and shattered ridges at the head of the valley. Although there seems little to connect these two summits, their traverse provides a fine full mountain day with an interesting low-grade straightforward scramble up the rock ridge of Y Gribin (the Gribin Ridge) to get you onto the tops quickly.

For a shorter round the beautiful amphitheatre of Cwm Idwal—worthy of a visit in its own right—and the famous cleft known as the 'Devil's Kitchen' (Twll Du) can be used as either a descent from Glyder Fawr or an ascent of Y Garn.

The route: Take the well constructed footpath which leaves the car park beside the little snack bar and toilet block. Go through the iron gate, cross the stream and follow the good path as it heads southwest with the west face of Tryfan rising ahead. In about 400m the path

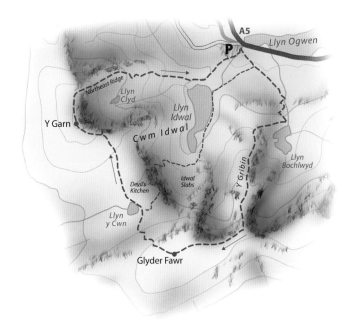

swings right towards Llyn Idwal. Don't follow the main path here take the path ahead which climbs steadily towards the gap between Tryfan and Glyder Fach. Higher up the path steepens beside the cascading stream flowing from Llyn Bochlwyd which remains out of sight until you reach level ground on the lip of the cwm.

Cwm Bochlwyd is a perfect example of a 'hanging valley', the floor of the cwm and the crag-lined headwall carved by a small glacier in a late glacial phase. Two famous ridges enclose this cwm—high up on the left is Bristly Ridge whilst the longer but gentler arm of Y Gribin encloses the right-hand side of the cwm.

Don't cross the stream here, turn right off the main path and follow a faint grassy trail (lake to the left) which becomes more obvious as you head towards the base of Y Gribin. At an obvious fork in the path bear left and follow the path, pitched here and there, up onto the blunt crest of the ridge. The ridge is rough but easy and the path well-used and obvious and leads, at a little over half-height, to a broad grassy shoulder large enough for a game of cricket. There are good views from here over to Tryfan and down into Cwm Idwal to the right.

Above, the ridge narrows into a rocky crest. The most interesting scrambling will be found on the crest of the ridge but there is some

Starting the scramble on the upper section of Y Gribin

exposure overlooking Cwm Bochlwyd. Easier, less interesting lines are always available to the right.

At the top of the ridge head rightwards along the edge of the cwm to reach the summit of Glyder Fawr, marked by a collection of rock spikes with superb views of the Snowdon group in clear conditions.

The continuation from Glyder Fawr is by a well-worn scree path which heads northwest and is marked regularly by cairns. Lower down this is steep and very loose and leads to the broad bwlch above the Devil's Kitchen where it joins the Idwal–Nant Peris path beside Llyn y Cŵn (a good reference point in mist). *To shorten the walk here see the final paragraph on page 71 and the description on page 72.*

(To reach this point via the Devil's Kitchen, take the pitched path from the car park at the eastern end of Llyn Ogwen to Llyn Idwal. Follow the path along the left-hand shore of the lake towards the clean sweep of rock known as the Idwal slabs. The path passes directly below the slabs which are often dotted with rock climbers. From here a stone-faced footpath veers right up the huge boulder field towards the dripping rocks of the famous Devil's Kitchen. Immediately below the gorge, the path bends left along a shattered terrace to reach Llyn y Cŵn ['lake of the dog']).

Follow the broad obvious path ahead past the lake *(right if you have come via the Devil's Kitched)*, then up the broad easy-angled stoney slopes which rise to Y Garn. As you near the shoulder of the mountain, the path follows the edge of the cwm to reach the summit.

From the summit walk north along the ridge until the obvious footpath can be seen dropping steeply down the northeast ridge. The path is quite steep and loose in places but easily followed. At about the halfway point the angle eases and you have a fine view into the cwm to Llyn Clyd on your right. Continue down the ridge which steepens again for a while to pass close to the shore of Llyn Idwal. Return can be made by the outgoing route from the end of the lake, but a better option is to look for a path which heads left about halfway along the lake to a stile in the fence. Cross the stile and continue ahead over grass to cross a second stile which leads down into a small man-made gorge to emerge in the car park again.

Llyn Bochlwyd

11. Glyder Fach & Glyder Fawr from Llyn Ogwen

Outline: *A good footpath takes you via the high mountain hollow of Cwm Bochlwyd to Bwlch Tryfan and up onto the Glyder plateau by the mountain's rounded eastern shoulder. Almost level walking across the plateau between the two summits gives superb views and allows the walker to enjoy the unusual rock architecture. Descent is by the famous Devil's Kitchen and Cwm Idwal where the fine rock scenery continues.*

Distance: *9.75km/6 miles.*

Height gained: *860m/2,820ft.*

Summits: *Glyder Fach & Glyder Fawr.*

Starting point: *Parking is available at the western end of Llyn Ogwen on the A5 and in lay-bys along the lake. Start the walk from the refreshment kiosk at the western end of the lake. Grid ref: SH 649 604.*

THE TWO GIANTS OF THE GLYDER RANGE stand shoulder to shoulder, separated by a wasteland of shattered rocks and tottering spikes, giving the summit plateau a lunar-like quality. To the south the land falls away gracefully to Dyffryn Mymbyr and the Llanberis Pass, but to the north things are very different—a landscape of deep glacial cwms separated by fine rock arêtes. These peaks are second only to Snowdon in their rugged grandeur.

Approaching from the north, this route avoids a direct frontal assault on the mountain, but still samples some of its fine rock scenery.

The route: Take the well-constructed footpath which leaves the car park beside the little snack bar. Where this turns right in about 400m to Cwm Idwal, keep ahead, soon rising more steeply beside the stream to reach the hanging valley of Cwm Bochlwyd with is sheltered lake. This path is known as the 'Miners' Track' and originated as the route taken by miners from Bethesda to reach the mines in Cwm Dyli on Snowdon.

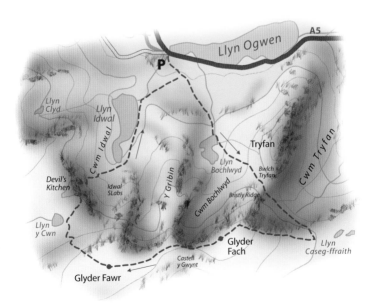

Stay with the 'Miners' Track' which continues ahead above the northeastern shore of the lake to Bwlch Tryfan. Cross the stone wall which straddles the bwlch and continue on the footpath ahead across scree to gain Glyder Fach's broad east ridge. Once you have gained the ridge turn sharp right up the final slopes—a mix of grass and jumbled rocks.

There are superb views of Tryfan to the right—its narrow summit ridge seen edge-on. A short detour to Llyn Caseg-fraith is worthwhile for the superb view of Tryfan with the lake in the foreground.

The summit of Glyder Fach is flat but far from unremarkable. Views southwest to Snowdon and north to Llyn Ogwen and Tryfan are superb and the summit plateau, with its chaotic rocks, can seem quite 'other worldly' particularly in misty conditions. The highest point—which can sometimes be difficult to decide on—lies just to the west of the famous rock table known as 'The Cantilever'.

Continue west across the plateau to the equally famous Castell y Gwynt—*'Castle of the Winds'*—a group of rock spikes 'as romantic

The west face of Tryfan from Llyn Bochlwyd passed en-route to Bwlch Tryfan

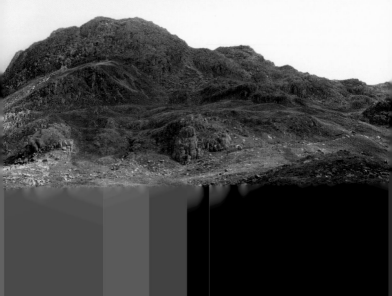

The steep descent from Glyder Fawr to Llyn y Cŵn

as their name'. The prospect of Snowdon with Castell y Gwynt in the foreground is one of Snowdonia's classic sights. The path skirts the rocks to the south (left) to regain the ridge where it narrows at Bwlch y Ddwy Glyder and there is a view down into Cwm Bochlwyd and across to Tryfan. From here a path rises to the right along the rim of Cwm Bochlwyd to the top of Y Gribin which could be used to shorten the route if needed, but involves scrambling (not recommended in bad conditions as the top of the ridge can be difficult to locate in poor visibility).

The path ahead continues to Glyder Fawr whose summit, like Glyder Fach, is marked by groups of jumbled rock formations providing mysterious foregrounds for views of the Snowdon group.

The usual descent from Glyder Fawr is by a well-worn scree path which heads northwest and is marked regularly by cairns. In its lower reaches this is very loose and leads to the broad bwlch above the Devil's Kitchen where it joins the Cwm Idwal–Nant Peris path beside Llyn y Cŵn. Turn right by the lake and follow the well constructed path steeply down beside the Devil's Kitchen into Cwm Idwal.

Lower down a short detour to the left will take you to the bottom of the 'Kitchen' itself. The unpleasant slippery rocks of the gorge were first climbed by Victorian pioneer rock climbers, but such dark, damp corners are avoided by modern rock gymnasts.

Below the Devils' Kitchen the path makes its way through a jumble of massive boulders. A fork in the path partway through the boulder field marks the divide between the paths which run along the eastern and western shores of Llyn Idwal. Take your pick here, both options are similar in length and terrain. The right-hand option will take you below the impressive rock face known as the Idwal Slabs returning along a formalised stone-faced path to Llyn Ogwen. The left-hand option offers the best views back into the cwm across the lake.

For the latter route, bear left at the fork and follow the path down through the boulders and along the eastern shore of Llyn Idwal. At the end of the lake go right along the shingle beach and cross the footbridge over the outflow. Turn left and follow the well-made footpath back to the car park.

The Devil's Kitchen rising above Llyn Idwal

A walker stands on The Cantilever with Snowdon in the distance

12. *Glyder Fach & Glyder Fawr from Pen-y-Gwryd*

Outline: *A quiet, little-used route up the southern slopes of Glyder Fawr with grand views of the Snowdon group, followed by easy walking across the Glyder plateau. Descent is by an easy-angled well-marked path. Sections around Llyn Cwmffynnon at the start of the walk can be very wet and boggy.*

Distance: *10.25km/6¼ miles.*

Height gained: *830m/2,720ft.*

Summits: *Glyder Fawr & Glyder Fach.*

Starting point: *There is a small lay-by immediately before Llyn Lockwood and beside the Pen-y-Gwryd Hotel, 6.5km/4 miles west of Capel Curig on the A4086. Grid ref: SH 665 559.*

IT MAY SEEM STRANGE TO SEEK OUT these featureless southern slopes, but the charm of this side of the mountain is the solitude and the superb views of Crib Goch and Crib y Ddysgl.

The route: There are two main options for the approach to Glyder Fawr's south ridge. A walk into Cwmffynnon with its lonely lake and stunning views of Crib Goch's east face, or a walk up the road to Pen-y-Pass. The main difficulty with the Cwmffynnon route is the boggy ground in the approaches to, and the walk around the lake (not recommended during, or shortly after heavy rain).

For the Cwmffynnon option, begin at the stile immediately to the east of the hotel and follow the obvious path ahead. After a footbridge and stile over the stream the path forks. Keep left here to a second stile in the fence. Follow the path which is often wet beside the fence and the stream. Where the fence ends turn left, cross the stream and head towards the outflow of the lake. Just before the shore turn right over a stile in the fence and walk around the northern shore of the lake.

Aim for the base of the ridge ahead and almost directly towards Crib Goch. There is a hollow on the ridge which is often boggy and from here you will be able to look down into the Llanberis Pass.

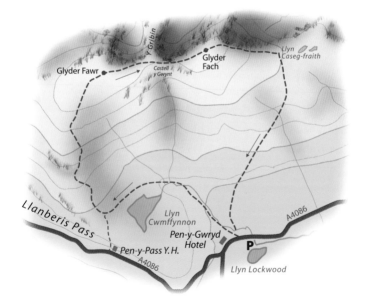

Looking south across the Moelwynion to Cadair Idris from Glyder Fawr

(This point can also be reached by walking up the road to Pen-y-Pass Youth Hostel and turning right through the gate on the signed footpath immediately beyond the buildings. Cross the wall by a stile and ascend quickly up onto the rounded ridge above. Head left along the ridge until it makes a short drop to the boggy area mentioned in the previous paragraph.)

From this point the ridge steepens into a series of broken crags separated by grass. The recognised route is marked by fading red blobs painted onto the rocks, but it is easy enough to pick your own route if you prefer. The best option is to keep within sight of Crib Goch's stunning east face over to your left, but be careful not to go too far left as higher up there are cliffs which overlook the pass.

Higher up you should reach a distinct col with one or two small pools and a prominent flat rock slab. Above this is a short steeper section, then the angle eases as you gain the summit plateau. Trend right from here aiming for the summit rock towers visible ahead.

Glyder Fawr is the highest of the two summits by just 4 metres and the walk between the two reflects this with just one small drop to the bwlch below Castell y Gwynt. In good visibility it is an enjoyable walk east along the edge of Cwm Cneifion (also known as 'Nameless Cwm') and Cwm Bochlwyd with the fine ridge of Y Gribin separating the two.

After a short drop to Bwlch y Ddwy-Glyder you can either take the easy scramble over Castell y Gwynt (*'Castle of the Winds'*) or the path which skirts the rocks to the right. The summit of Glyder Fach lies 200-300m further east.

East of the summit is the famous rock table known as 'The Cantilever'. Pass this on the left following the path east along the upper edge of Cwm Tryfan. Take care not to follow the path which bears left and descends within about 350m of the summit beside Bristly Ridge. The correct path descends gently southeast to the broad grass bwlch beside the pools of Llyn y Caseg-fraith.

Once you are off the scree and onto the grass and about 300m before the pools, look for a path on the right. This is known as the 'Miner's Track' and was used by miners travelling between the mines on Snowdon and Bethesda. You will see the continuation of this path bending leftwards to Bwlch Tryfan at the foot of Bristly Ridge.

Turn right here and follow the path over almost level grass passing to the right of a rocky knoll. The path should be clear now and can be followed easily down the gentle hillside to finish at the Pen-y-Gwryd Hotel, visible down in the valley.

The view to Tryfan from Llyn Caseg-fraith

Senior's Ridge, Glyder Fawr and Y Gribin from Nant Ffrancon

13. Senior's Ridge, Glyder Fawr & Y Gribin

Outline: **SCRAMBLE** *An easy walk on a good path to the sheltered mountain lake of Llyn Bochlwyd. A contouring path then leads with minimal effort around the steep slopes of Y Gribin and high above Llyn Idwal to the hidden valley of Cwm Cneifion. From here a rarely visited, broken ridge offers low-grade, interesting scrambling to the Glyder plateau. Return is made by the fine rock arête of Y Gribin.*

Distance: *7.25km/4¼ miles.*

Height gained: *744m/2,440ft.*

Summits: *Glyder Fawr.*

Starting point: *Parking is available at the western end of Llyn Ogwen and in lay-bys along the lake. Start the walk from the snack bar. Grid ref: SH 649 604.*

THIS SUPERB ROUTE IS ONE OF THE BEST KEPT SECRETS of the Glyderau and once the approach to Cwm Bochlwyd is behind you, you are likely to have the mountain to yourself (not recommended in poor visibility).

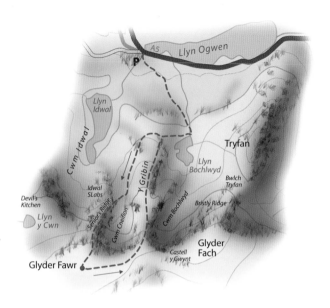

The route: Take the well-constructed footpath which leaves the car park beside the little snack bar. Where this turns right in about 400m to Cwm Idwal, keep ahead, soon rising more steeply beside the stream to the hanging valley of Cwm Bochlwyd.

As the path levels and the northern cliffs of Glyder Fach come into view across Llyn Bochlwyd, turn right along the north shore of the lake. There are one or two faint paths here but a good path becomes established as you reach the base of Y Gribin. Don't turn left on the stone paved path up the ridge here, instead continue ahead. In about 150m the path splits—bear left (the route ahead leads down to Llyn Idwal). A narrow but well-defined contouring footpath now takes you effortlessly across steep slopes high above Llyn Idwal with superb views across the cwm to Y Garn and the impressive rock scenery of the Devil's Kitchen and Idwal Slabs.

As you near the rocky shoulder of Senior's Ridge you discover one of the hidden gems of this route—the hanging valley of Cwm Cneifion, tucked away in the folds of the mountain and virtually invisible from below. The floor of the cwm is almost flat and carpeted in springy turf. The only disappointment is that there is no mountain lake here as there is in the adjacent cwm.

Cross the cwm to join the broad rounded ridge which rises as a series of rocky bluffs similar to Tryfan's North Ridge (but without the crowds!). The broken ridge leads directly onto the summit plateau leaving an easy walk to the group of rocks marking the highest point.

From the summit walk east along the ridge towards Glyder Fach. Soon you will be looking down into Cwm Cneifion with the rocky crest of Y Gribin ahead. Follow the edge of the cwm to the top of the ridge. This can be difficult to locate in poor visibility, the main problem being to distinguish the initial steep section of the ridge from the broken slabby rocks which bound the eastern side of Cwm Cneifion. Despite appearances the ridge is straightforward with the best scrambling on the ridge crest. Easier, less exposed options can be found on the broken slabby ground to the left.

The rocks end on a broad shoulder, large and flat enough for a putting green and a good path leads back down to Llyn Bochlwyd. Retrace the outward route back to Ogwen.

The rock ridge of Y Gribin and Cwm Cneifion seen from Nant Ffrancon

The East Face of Tryfan showing Heather Terrace

14. *Tryfan via Heather Terrace, the South Ridge & Cwm Tryfan*

Outline: *Although it looks dramatic, this is one of the easiest routes on the mountain and finds its way across the massive East Face by means of a broad rocky terrace. Rock scenery is impressive for much of the ascent. There is a little scrambling here and there and just one short section near the summit where there is some unavoidable exposure. Return is by the South Ridge and Cwm Tryfan.*

Distance: *6.5km/4 miles.*

Height gained: *699m/2,300ft.*

Summits: *Tryfan.*

Starting point: *There is a lay-by on the A5 at the eastern end of Llyn Ogwen between the lake and the track to Gwern Gof Uchaf farm. Grid ref: SH 671 605.*

THIS SUPERB ROCK PEAK IS OFF-LIMITS to anyone not prepared to use their hands as well as their feet to reach its summit. By the easiest route

(South Ridge) there are just one or two places where you will need to take your hands out of your pockets, but care is still needed, particularly in descent. This route uses Heather Terrace—the distinctive rake which runs below the East Face of the mountain—to reach the South Ridge which gives the easiest approach to the summit.

The route: Walk east along the A5 and turn right down the track to Gwern Gof Uchaf farm. Follow the track to the farm passing it on the left-hand side where a stile leads over the wall onto a bridleway (previously the old road through the valley). Turn right along the bridleway for a few metres to a point level with the farm outbuildings and bear left on a footpath which heads towards Tryfan. Ignore a left turn at a fork in the path continuing ahead, then walk up past the prominent rock slab known as 'Little Tryfan'. Immediately after the slab the path bears right up over small rock ribs to a stile over the fence giving access to the Cwm Tryfan path. Don't cross this stile, instead, take the path to the right and walk up parallel to the fence. Higher up the path rises by stone steps through a short gully.

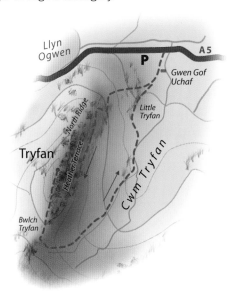

At the top of the gully take the path immediately on the left which leads onto Heather Terrace. The path along the terrace is well used and can be followed comfortably. The rock scenery is also superb as you pass below the impressive buttresses of the East Face.

At the end of Heather Terrace, turn steeply up a broad, short scree slope which leads onto the South Ridge of the mountain. Cross the stile over the wall and follow the path rightwards up the broad rocky ridge to the summit marked by the twin rocks of 'Adam and Eve'.

To descend retrace your route down the broad South Ridge passing the Heather Terrace Path where you crossed the wall and continuing to Bwlch Tryfan separating Tryfan from Glyder Fach. Cross the stile over the wall on the left at the lowest point on the bwlch and take the path across the head of Cwm Tryfan. Before you reach the broad shoulder ahead look for an obvious footpath on the left which takes a direct line down Cwm Tryfan below the towering East Face of the mountain.

Cross a stile in the fence above Little Tryfan and follow the path down to Gwern Gof Uchaf to complete the round.

Tryfan and Cwm Tryfan showing Heather Terrace below the East Face and the path down Cwm Tryfan

The East Face of Tryfan rising above Cwm Tryfan

15. *Tryfan—East Face, South Ridge & Braich Ddeugwm*

Outline: SCRAMBLE *This route takes the easier sections of the North Ridge and avoids the harder scrambling higher up by traversing the gullies of the East Face. Short sections of moderate scrambling are required on the North Ridge and in the gullies near the summit. Descent is by the easier South Ridge, followed by straightforward walking around the rim of Cwm Tryfan with superb views of Tryfan's East Face.*

Distance: *8km/5 miles.*

Height gained: *750m/2,450ft.*

Summits: *Tryfan.*

Starting point: *There is a lay-by on the A5 just to the east of Llyn Ogwen between the lake and the track to Gwern Gof Uchaf farm. Grid ref: SH 671 605.*

TRYFAN IS ARGUABLY THE FINEST MOUNTAIN IN SNOWDONIA. A true rock peak, it stands apart from the main bulk of the Glyder range like a giant up-turned axe blade and has delighted travellers west-bound on the A5 for centuries. Few can forget their first sight of it as its great rock towers slide into view from behind the rounded, unremarkable shoulder of Gallt yr Ogof.

Which ever route you take to the summit you will not be able to avoid using your hands here and there. This route follows the famous North Ridge but avoids the hardest section by turning into the gullies on the East Face where scrambling is easier and less exposed.

The route: Walk east along the A5 and turn right down the track to Gwern Gof Uchaf farm. Follow the track to the farm passing it on the left-hand side where a stile leads over the wall onto a bridleway (previously the old road through the valley). Turn right along the bridleway for a few metres to a point level with the farm outbuildings and bear left on a footpath which heads towards Tryfan. Ignore a left turn at a fork in the path continuing ahead, then bear left up past the prominent rock slab known as 'Little Tryfan'. Immediately after the slab the path bears right up over small rock ribs to a stile over the fence giving access to the Cwm Tryfan path. Don't cross this stile, instead, take the path to the right and walk up parallel to the fence. Higher up the path rises by stone steps through a short gully.

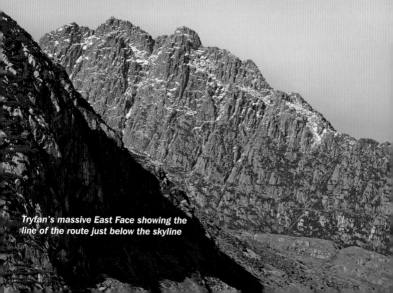

Tryfan's massive East Face showing the line of the route just below the skyline

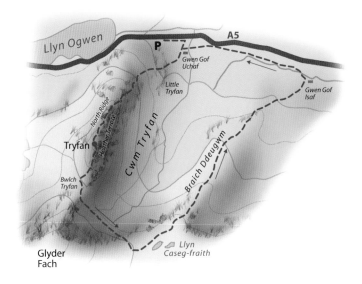

At the top of the gully don't take the path immediately left which leads onto Heather Terrace, instead, continue ahead a little further onto the shoulder of the mountain. You are now at the foot of the famous North Ridge which can be tackled by a number of lines—the easiest follows a ribbon of scree and boulders directly below the broken ridge crest above. All routes converge at a broad shoulder with distinctive flat rock slabs.

Above the shoulder, the ridge continues broken and indistinct to a second level area, smaller this time but with similar flat rock slabs. Above lies a much steeper pyramidal buttress. The North Ridge route tackles this buttress direct, but the East Face route (which is a little easier and less exposed) turns this obstacle on the left to begin a traverse of the gullies.

The path rises leftwards well below the crest of the North Ridge and requires some scrambling. The path now traverses the upper section of the first gully, then scrambles up to reach a notch immediately below the North Peak. Continue across the gully beyond the notch where a similar scramble brings you to the summit beside the famous twin rocks known as 'Adam and Eve'.

Descend the South Ridge passing the South Peak over to the left and cross the small bwlch to Far South Peak (wall over to the left). Continue the descent to Bwlch Tryfan—the watershed between Cwm Tryfan and Cwm Bochlwyd—where there is another wall. Ahead rise the rocks of Bristly Ridge and the northern cliffs of Glyder Fach. The 'Miners' Track', a path linking the mines on Snowdon with Bethesda, crosses the bwlch here at its lowest point and continues across the screes to the left to reach the rounded shoulder of Glyder Fach. Follow this path left over the wall and across to the shoulder. Once on the skyline bear left to the scattering of small lakes (Llyn Caseg-fraith) to locate the top of Braich y Ddeugwm, the long finger-like ridge forming the eastern bounds of Cwm Tryfan.

There is a footpath here but it is faint and could be very difficult to find in poor visibility. In good visibility no path is needed—once on the ridge the walking is a delight with springy turf underfoot and stunning views across Cwm Tryfan to the East Face of Tryfan and Bristly Ridge.

The ridge ends above Gwern Gof Isaf farm. Walk past the farm and down the access track towards the road. Just before the bridge turn left along the right of way which follows the line of the old road through the valley back to Gwern Gof Uchaf farm.

(A shorter route from the summit of Tryfan can be made by returning via Heather Terrace—the prominent terrace which crosses the mountain below the East Face. For this option follow the South Ridge to the bwlch between the South Peak and Far South Peak. Cross the stile over the wall here and descend the scree which falls into Cwm Tryfan. About halfway down the scree look for a cairned path on the left (easily missed). This marks the end of Heather Terrace, the feature which is so obvious from the valley but not so obvious when you are trying to locate it. Follow the path along the terrace which soon becomes better established. The terrace eventually leads to the short gully used on the ascent at the foot of the North Ridge. Bear right down the gully and return via Little Tryfan to Gwern Gof Uchaf farm.)

Looking directly up Tryfan's North Ridge

16. *The Bochlwyd Horseshoe*

Outline: SCRAMBLE *Scrambling starts low down on Tryfan's North Ridge. Higher up two fine rock pitches take you onto the North Peak and finally the airy summit. After a descent of the easier and shorter South Ridge, the pinnacles of Bristly Ridge deliver you onto the rocky summit plateau of Glyder Fach. The impressive rock scenery continues with the famous Cantilever and Castell y Gwynt. Descent is by the rock ridge of Y Gribin completing the circuit of Cwm Bochlwyd.*

Distance: *6.5km/4 miles.*

Height gained: *930m/3,080ft.*

Summits: *Tryfan & Glyder Fach (Glyder Fawr optional).*

Starting point: *Car park or lay-bys at the eastern end of Llyn Ogwen. Begin directly below the large bulging buttress of rock (known as the 'Milestone Buttress') which has a stone wall reaching from its lowest rocks down to the road.*
Grid ref: SH 663 603.

THIS IS A SUPERB ROUTE COMBINING THE IMPRESSIVE rock ridges of Tryfan and Glyder Fach. For quality of scrambling and purity of line the Bochlwyd Horseshoe can only be rivalled (and arguably not exceeded) by the Snowdon Horseshoe. The crest of Bristly Ridge provides the crux of the scrambling and there are one or two exposed sections where care is needed. Once this is behind you, you can stride out and enjoy the remaining rock scenery in the form of 'The Cantilever' and Castell y Gwynt (*'Castle of the Winds'*) seen against an impressive back drop of the Snowdon group. Descent is by the easier but still interesting rock ridge of Y Gribin (Gribin Ridge).

The route: From the road take the footpath on the left side of the wall leading up to the Milestone Buttress. Directly below the crag, turn left on a pitched path which rises to the rounded ridge crest below an indistinct rock step on the right. This is the foot of the North Ridge proper.

Take your pick of numerous routes which tackle the broken rocks above. The easiest and most straightforward follows a ribbon of scree and boulders directly below the broken ridge crest above (looking directly up the ridge). More challenging lines can be found to the right, but don't stray too far from the crest. All routes converge at a broad shoulder with distinctive flat rock slabs.

'The Cannon' on Tryfan's North Ridge

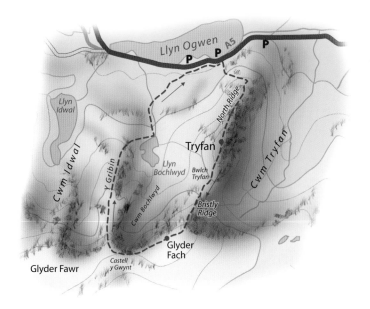

Unusual rock formations are very much the theme on this route and part-way up this section you will pass the first of several. Known as 'The Cannon', walkers have been climbing and photographing each other on this angled rock slab since Victorian times.

All routes converge at a broad flat shoulder with distinctive flat rock slabs. Above, the ridge continues broad and broken to a second shoulder, smaller this time but with similar rock slabs. Above lies a much steeper pyramidal buttress. (*There is an escape route to the left here which takes you across the shattered East Face at an easier grade, but the route still requires scrambling—see the previous route.*) Back to the North Ridge and the best scrambling is to be found taking a direct line up the pyramidal buttress with easier options to the right.

The next obstacle is the large tower of the North Peak. A direct ascent is not an option but a wide easy chimney to the right delivers you onto the summit. Move easily across the connecting ridge to the

The rocks of Castell y Gwynt with Snowdon behind

main summit of the mountain where you will encounter the next rock curiosity of the day, the twin stones known as 'Adam and Eve'. They are the sole remnants of a layer of rock which has been removed leaving these two pillars standing like the final teeth in a decaying jaw.

This is a fine mountain summit, a small rock shelf poised above the huge East Face and not a blade of grass anywhere. Possibly the best summit in Snowdonia

Descend the South Ridge by a choice of routes—the main path keeps to the right of the South Peak and away from the East Face but more scrambling can be enjoyed by staying close to the crest of the ridge.

At Bwlch Tryfan you can prepare yourself for the climax of the day—one of Snowdonia's finest scrambles—Bristly Ridge. From the bwlch follow the path on the right side of the wall which rises up to the lowest rocks of the ridge above. The path soon bears diagonally-right up the scree to the foot of the rocks. There is a prominent gully above at this point. Ignore this bearing left. About 10m from the wall turn right up a short chimney with a section of wall at the top. Climb over this and turn right up a chimney above. Where the climbing becomes hard move onto the left wall, then move back right across the chimney to a rib which leads up to easier ground.

Continue directly up the ridge to the first small pinnacle, cross the gap and continue up to the second much larger pinnacle. The descent into the next gap can look quite intimidating. It is easier than it looks but still requires care. Climb down into the gap from the left. Pass to the right of a huge flake of rock to reach a recess behind. Climb the corner and move right onto steeper rocks to reach easier ground. The easy ridge above delivers you onto the summit plateau.

A short walk across the lunar-like landscape of the plateau will take you to the summit.

A stone's throw from the highest rocks is the famous rock table known as 'The Cantilever'. Unless you have the mountain to yourself (very rare!) there will be the usual gathering taking photographs of each other standing on the table. Even Thomas Pennant couldn't resist this over 200 years ago. His artist produced a drawing little different from the images taken home by today's walkers.

From the summit continue west along the broad ridge to another group of rocks almost as famous as 'The Cantilever'—Castell y Gwynt. A path avoids the rocks on the south side but taken direct they provide pleasant scrambling. Rejoin the path on the far side where it forks;

Looking back to Glyder Fach and Castell y Gwynt from the top of Y Gribin

bear right here (the path ahead continues to Glyder Fawr, a short out-and-back walk if you are in summit bagging mode) making a short rise along the edge of Cwm Bochlwyd to the top of Y Gribin (Gribin Ridge). In poor visibility it is not always easy to locate the top of the ridge as the first few metres are quite steep and look little different to the slabs tumbling into Cwm Cneifion. In normal conditions however there should be no problem. The best scrambling is to be found near the crest with easier lines to the left.

Things become easier as you descend until the ridge widens and levels. There are superb views across Cwm Bochlwyd to Tryfan and down into Cwm Cneifion from here.

At the foot of the ridge (almost level with Llyn Bochlwyd) turn right at a crossing path (the path to the left leads down to Llyn Idwal) and follow the path to the outflow of Llyn Bochlwyd where you will meet the 'Miners' Track'—a broad obvious footpath once used by miners from Bethesda to reach the mines on Snowdon. Turn left and follow the 'Miners' Track' steeply down beside the stream. As the angle eases a faint path bears right. This path heads across the lower slopes of Tryfan to the eastern end of Llyn Ogwen to complete the route.

On Y Gribin at the end of the scrambling

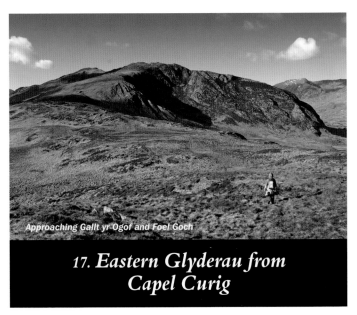

Approaching Gallt yr Ogof and Foel Goch

17. Eastern Glyderau from Capel Curig

Outline: *A short moderate ascent onto a broad grass ridge which is then followed with stunning views in clear conditions to the neglected Gallt yr Ogof. Easy, elevated walking over Y Foel Goch leads to the beautiful pools of Llyn Caseg-fraith with their stunning views of Tryfan. Return is by the easy ridge of Braich y Ddeugwm to Gwern Gof Isaf, then along the a bridleway back to Capel Curig.*

Distance: *12.25km/7½ miles.*

Height gained: *719m/2,360ft.*

Summits: *Gallt yr Ogof & Y Foel Goch (could be extended to include Glyder Fach & Glyder Fawr).*

Starting point: *Free, limited parking is available behind the shops in Capel Curig. Grid ref: SH 720 583. Alternatively, the walk could be started at Gwern Gof Isaf where a small charge is made for parking. Grid ref: SH 685 602.*

Tryfan from Llyn Caseg-fraith

THE MAIN DRAMA OF THE GLYDERAU LIES IN ITS CENTRAL HEIGHTS which surround Llyn Idwal and Llyn Ogwen with the result that the northwestern and eastern ends of the range lie neglected. Poor Gallt yr Ogof, anywhere else and this mountain would be celebrated, but standing in the shadow of Tryfan what chance does it have?

Fortunately, as is often the case, Gallt yr Ogof is a superb viewpoint and it would be hard to imagine a more enjoyable walk than striding the easy-angled ridge from Capel Curig on a clear warm day, the pinnacles of Snowdon ahead; Moel Siabod to the left reflected in the waters of Llynnau Mymbyr; the rounded shoulders of the Carneddau across the Ogwen valley to the right and as you reach the summit ridge you have the great finale of Tryfan's rock buttresses set against a foreground of sparkling pools. Enough said?

The route: From the car park go right along the old road. In 200m or so pass a house on the left and a little further on take the faint path on the left which climbs directly weaving between small slabby crags (Creigiau'r Gelli) to gain the crest of the ridge above (Cefn y Capel). A

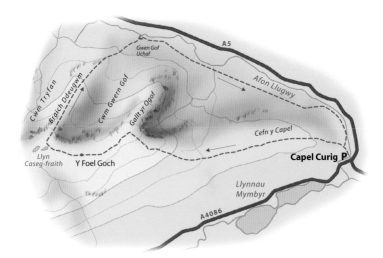

good, almost level footpath now heads west along the broad ridge, the easy walking allowing you to fully enjoy the stunning views.

Contine to Bwlch Goleuni, then rise more steeply up onto the shoulder beyond a stile. Higher up the path swings left taking a diagonal line to the broad flat bwlch between Gallt yr Ogof and Y Foel Goch where Tryfan's huge East Face comes into view. Gallt yr Ogof lies on an out-and-back detour a few hundred metres to the right. From the bwlch a short rise leads to the rather nonedescript top of Y Foel Goch and a gentle descent brings you to the handful of pools known as Llyn Caseg-fraith. These make a superb foreground for one of the best views of Tryfan, particularly in the early morning.

For a return to Capel Curig you could retrace your route back along the ridge, but the only real option for a circular walk is to descend to Gwern Gof Isaf farm in the Ogwen valley to the right. It would be possibe to descend via Cwm Tryfan but a far better option is by the rarely used Braich y Ddeugwm, the easy-angled grassy ridge separating Cwm Tryfan and Cwm Gwern Gof.

From Llyn Caseg-fraith head northeast to gain the top of the ridge and follow it easily down to Gwern Gof Isaf. The interest is maintained on the descent by the stunning views of Tryfan. At the farm walk down the access track towards the A5 but just before the bridge turn right onto the bridleway which follows what remains of the old road through the valley. This leads back to Capel Curig—about 3.5km/2¼ miles.

Snowdon, Crib Goch and Crib y Ddysgl from Llynnau Mymbyr

Snowdon/Yr Wyddfa

The Snowdon Horseshoe from Llynnau Mymbyr, Capel Curig

Snowdon/Yr Wyddfa

FROM ANY APPROACH SNOWDON DEMANDS ATTENTION—its height, architectural complexity and dramatic skylines dominate the whole of northern Snowdonia. Even the height and closeness of its neighbours takes nothing away from this great mountain. If you were to place it amongst the giants of the Scottish Higlands it would still stand proud and aloof. The prospect of its four main summits—Y Lliwedd, Yr Wyddfa (Snowdon), Crib Goch and Crib y Ddysgl (better known as the 'Snowdon Horseshoe') mirrored in the calm waters of Llynnau Mymbyr at Capel Curig, is one of the great mountain views of Britain.

Snowdon is not just one mountain of course, but a group of peaks—a massif—all high, all fine mountain summits in themselves, yet the central summit of Yr Wyddfa reigns supreme. And it is fitting that Snowdon's crowning glory should be located at this central point—the meeting of five fine ridges radiating to all points of the compass and rising at the head of three wild mountain cwms.

But Snowdon does have its down side. As the highest mountain in England, Ireland and Wales, it was the focus of great interest and activity throughout the Victorian period when it became fashionable to spend the night on its summit to view the sunrise the following morning. To accommodate these visitors, an assortment of huts and 'hotels' were built during the nineteenth century and guides could be hired for the ascent. In 1896 the now famous Snowdon Mountain Railway was built—the buildings and engineering work associated with it, adding further scars to an increasingly 'urbanised' summit. The result of this is that today over 300,000 visitors reach its summit each year and at times it is one of the most crowded places in Snowdonia. But Snowdon is a big mountain and with a little thought and route planning the crowds can be avoided even in the height of the season.

The group is enclosed by a triangle of three main roads. To the north the A4086 descends from Pen-y-Pass through the jaws of the Llanberis Pass to the town of Llanberis and beside its two lakes—Llyn Padarn and Llyn Peris. To the southeast the A498 weaves through the wooded vale of Nantgwynant and beside the lovely Llyn Gwynant and Llyn Dinas to the tiny village of Beddgelert. The third side of the triangle is formed by the A4085 which heads north from Beddgelert beside Nant Colwyn and the extensive plantations of the Beddgelert Forest, through the village of Rhyd-Ddu and along the shore of Llyn Cwellyn towards Caernarfon. Included in this area are a number of lower summits which lie along a ridge extending northwest from Bwlch Brwynog—Moel Eilio, Foel Goch and Moel Cynghorion.

The Snowdon Horseshoe from Llynnau Mymbyr

The summit of Snowdon can sometimes be one of the busiest places in Snowdonia

Snowdon from the southwest (Rhyd-Ddu Path), with the South Ridge on the right

Snowdon probably has more routes to its summit than any other mountain in Britain. There are six 'Classic Paths'—well established routes, constructed for much of their length and the majority have been in use for well over a century.

The longest and easiest begins at Llanberis and more or less follows the railway. This has become the 'tourist route' and receives by far the most 'traffic', but it is probably the least interesting way to the summit. Llanberis is also the best starting point for Snowdon's northerly outliers from Moel Cynghorion to Moel Eilio.

The oldest route is said to be the Snowdon Ranger Path which begins at the Youth Hostel of the same name on the shores of Llyn Cwellyn to the west. A similar approach begins at Rhyd-Ddu a little further south. These two starting points can now be linked by the Welsh Highland Railway.

The Watkin Path lays claim to being the prettiest route, beginning in the woods of Nantgwynant to the south, but this approach involves the most height gain, having the lowest starting point.

Looking into Cwm Dyli from Crib y Ddysgl

The most dramatic and impressive approach is undoubtedly from the east via Cwm Dyli. Despite a constructed mining road and mining spoil along the way, Cwm Dyli—enclosed by the knife edge crest of Crib Goch and the 300m face of Y Lliwedd—is probably the most dramatic mountain valley outside Scotland. The two paths known as the Pyg Track and the Miner's Track start from Pen-y-Pass and can be combined, the latter route providing the best descent.

In addition to the 'Classic Paths' there are a number of less frequented or more adventurous routes. The best known of these and one of the finest mountain days to be enjoyed in Snowdonia is the Snowdon Horseshoe. This traverses the narrow ridges enclosing Cwm Dyli including the famous Crib Goch. This exposed, narrow rock ridge will either be a wonderful introduction to the delights of scrambling or the pinnacle of achievement for the less adventurous.

An alternative and less exposed horseshoe walk can be made from Nantgwynant encircling Cwm Llan by an ascent of Y Lliwedd and a descent of Snowdon's South Ridge. This option avoids the 'horrors' of Crib Goch if exposed scrambling is not your thing.

The best side of the mountain to avoid the crowds is to the north where the hanging valley of Cwm Glas Mawr and Cwm Uchaf sit high above the Llanberis Pass. There was an old route from Pen-y-Pass which passed this way but its line is very faint and veering from the constructed Pyg Track is now discouraged. A fine scrambling route of similar standard to the Snowdon Horseshoe can be made from this side of the mountain by way of Crib Goch's North Ridge, followed by a traverse of the Crib Goch/Crib y Ddysgl ridge and a descent of the little-used Gyrn Lâs Ridge which leads back into the Llanberis Pass. For the competent scrambler this is one of the best routes on the mountain.

The 'pinnacles' of Crib Goch overlooking the wilds of Cwm Glas

Snowdon and the Llanberis Ridge

18. *Snowdon from Llanberis* — *The Llanberis Ridge*

Outline: *This route stays within sight of both the Snowdon Mountain Railway and the Llanberis Path, but distances itself sufficiently to avoid the crowds once the initial approach is over. Thereafter you will have one of the longest ridges on the mountain almost to yourself and you will be able to enjoy stunning views into the Llanberis Pass which remain hidden from the hordes on the tourist route.*

Distance: *18.5km/11½ miles.*

Height gained: *1,470m/4,825ft.*

Summits: *Crib y Ddysgl, Snowdon & Moel Cynghorion.*

Starting point: *Llanberis is busy during the summer months when the railway is in operation. There is plenty of parking space opposite the Snowdon Mountain Railway in Llanberis, but during the high season car parks become very crowded, so you need to get there early. Grid ref: SH 582 599. Alternative parking is available at Nant Peris Park and Ride. Grid ref: SH 606 583.*

THE LLANBERIS PATH IS THE EASIEST WAY of reaching the summit of Snowdon and as such is the most popular and most crowded route on the mountain. In the lower two thirds it also manages to avoid any interest at all. However, just a stone's throw away is the Llanberis Ridge, the mountain's northern arm. An ascent of this ridge is far more rewarding both for spectacular views and avoiding the crowds.

The route: The Llanberis Path starts its long monotonous climb from 'Victoria Terrace', the road directly opposite the 'Royal Victoria Hotel', on the Nant Peris road out of Llanberis. Beyond the houses cross the cattle grid and follow the steeply rising lane, with the Snowdon Mountain Railway on your right.

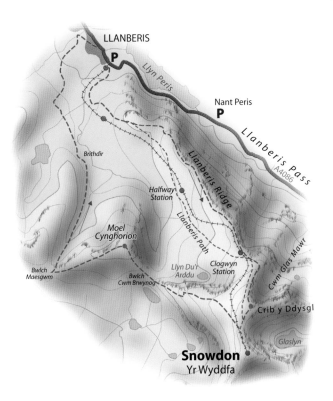

At the top of the road go through the gate by 'Pen Ceunant Uchaf' on the right and about 200m further on turn left onto the signed footpath.

In about 500m break away from the broad path and head left up grass with no path to gain the ridge. After the first top the ridge dips slightly to a broad grass col. The climb becomes much steeper now in the rise to a second minor top. There is a faint path close to the fence here.

Looking up the Llanberis Ridge towards Crib Goch, Crib y Ddysgl and Snowdon

The hard work is over for a while and you can now enjoy the undulating ridge ahead with impressive views into the Llanberis Pass and down to Nant Peris on your left.

As you approach the rocky summit of Llechog, purists will follow the ridge and then descend to its junction with the railway but this can be avoided by walking beside the railway which runs almost along the crest of the ridge to the Clogwyn Station, where you will also meet the Llanberis Path. The Llanberis Path provides the easiest route from here to the summit of Snowdon, but the most interesting route follows the edge of the steep cwm on your left to the top of the Gyrn Lâs Ridge which drops steeply into the Llanberis Pass.

From here you are treated to a superb view ahead across upper Cwm Glas Mawr and Cwm Uchaf to the rocky nose of Clogwyn y Person and the Crib Goch pinnacles.

Turn right up the edge of the cwm to the summit of Crib y Ddysgl. In clear conditions Snowdon will be visible ahead and the way obvious—a short descent southwest takes you to Bwlch Glas where there is a 2-metre upright stone marking the point where the Pyg Track and Miners' Track reach the ridge. From here there is an easy ten minute walk beside the railway to the summit of Snowdon. (On Crib y Ddysgl take care not to accidently follow the ridge eastwards in poor visibility).

The easiest and simplest descent is by the Llanberis Path which you will have seen close by on the ascent.

A more interesting route is to descend the upper section of the Snowdon Ranger Path, which bears northwest (left) away from the railway at the 2-metre upright stone on Bwlch Glas. Take care in poor visibility as you approach the massive cliffs of Clogwyn Du'r Arddu. Descend the zig-zag path beside the crags to Bwlch Cwm Brwynog, then ascend the ridge ahead to Moel Cynghorion. Follow the broad grassy ridge southwest to Bwlch Maesgwm.

Turn right (north) onto a path (thought to be an ancient packhorse trail) and follow this for 3km/1¾ miles passing the farmhouse of 'Brithdir' to a lane on the right at GR. 574 591 ('Ffordd Capel Coch'). Turn right and follow the lane past the Youth Hostel back to Llanberis.

Approaching Bwlch Cwm Brwynog on the Snowdon Ranger Path

19. Snowdon from the west— Snowdon Ranger/Rhyd-Ddu Path

Outline: *The early stages of the walk can be wet as you negotiate the boggy ground below Cwm Clogwyn before a rise is made close to, but out of sight of, the huge cliffs of Clogwyn Du'r Arddu. The final section is shared with the Llanberis Path and the Snowdon Mountain Railway. Descent is by the upper section of the South Ridge across the narrows of Bwlch Main, followed by a long gradual descent over rock and grass to Rhyd-Ddu.*

Distance: *14km/8¾ miles.*

Height gained: *1,050m/3,350ft.*

Summits: *Snowdon (Yr Wyddfa).*

Starting point: *There is a car park opposite the Snowdon Ranger Youth Hostel on the A4085 (grid ref: SH 565 551) or park at Rhyd-Ddu (grid ref: SH 571 527) and take the train to Snowdon Ranger.*

THIS ROUTE PROVIDES A CIRCUIT OF CWM CLOGWYN, probably the least impressive of the mountain's five great cwms, but there will be drama enough on the upper slopes as you pass above the precipice of Clogwyn Du'r Arddu and on the narrow South Ridge as you cross Bwlch Main (known as 'The Saddle'). On the descent return to Snowdon Ranger can be made either by a 2km/1¼ mile walk along the road or by the Welsh Highland Railway.

The Snowdon Ranger Path is perhaps the easiest route to the summit after the Llanberis Path and is believed to be the oldest, being named after John Morton who called himself the 'Snowdon Ranger' and used to guide Victorian gentlemen up the mountain.

The route: Cross the road and take the signed footpath and bridleway almost opposite beside the driveway to 'Caer Orsaf'. Cross the track of the Welsh Highland Railway turning left and then right up the track to 'Llwyn Onn farm'. Above the farm the path zig-zags up the hillside gaining height quickly.

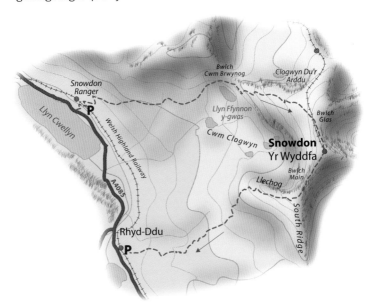

After a gate in a wall the angle eases and the path crosses flatter more boggy ground. The ridge can be seen rising ahead and there are good views into Cwm Clogwyn to the right.

The path rises almost to the bwlch on the left and above the waters of Llyn Ffynnon-y-gwas. A short diversion to the bwlch gives a fine view into Cwm Brwynog and in the distance the Llanberis Path. From here the path begins to zig-zag up onto the ridge above. This is the toughest section of the climb but it is soon over. Higher up, the ridge narrows as you approach the top of the cliffs of Clogwyn Du'r Arddu.

If you have a good head for heights go to your left a little and have a look at this awesome 200m precipice where some of the most serious rock climbs in North Wales have been pioneered.

Returning to the path, continue the climb until the angle eases and the path widens into a broad stoney plateau. The going now becomes much easier and soon you swing right to cross the Snowdon Mountain Railway and join the Llanberis Path at the 2-metre upright stone on

The final section of the Snowdon Ranger Path with the summit in sight

Snowdon showing the South Ridge and the Rhyd-Ddu Path used in descent

Bwlch Glas with its stunning views into Cwm Dyli. From here it is about another ten minutes or so beside the railway to the summit.

From the summit head south, initially along the upper section of the South Ridge with grand views down into Cwm Llan in clear conditions. Soon the ridge narrows and levels at Bwlch Main (known as 'The Saddle'). An interesting short narrow section follows with views into both Cwm Clogwyn to the right and Cwm Tregalen on the left. There is a small subsidiary top on the southern side of the bwlch and just before this the path forks. The South Ridge route continues ahead and the Rhyd -Ddu Path bears right along the crag-lined rim of Cwm Clogwyn.

Soon you pass through a stone wall and swing left across the broad rounded shoulder of Llechog to pass through the wall again. The path is now well worn and can be followed easily to its junction with the track leading from Rhyd-Ddu to Bwlch Cwm Llan at the foot of the South Ridge. Turn right along this track and follow it to the Rhyd-Ddu car park. Turn right and follow the road back to Snowdon Ranger (2km/1¼ miles) or catch a train on the Welsh Highland Railway.

Snowdon (Yr Wyddfa), Crib Goch and Crib y Ddysgl enclosing the dramatic Cwm Dyli

20. Snowdon from the east—Pyg Track/Miners' Track

Outline: *A gradual climb along a rocky, well constructed path leads to Bwlch Moch. From here you enter the Snowdon Horseshoe with its grand scenery. Old mine workings add extra interest, before the final climb up the famous 'Zig-zags' to join the Snowdon Mountain Railway and the Llanberis Path, which is followed to the summit. Descent is by a return down the 'Zig-zags' and a steep rocky path to Glaslyn and Llyn Llydaw. The remains of an old mining road are used to return to Pen-y-Pass.*

Distance: *12km/7½ miles.*

Height gained: *914m/3,000ft.*

Summits: *Snowdon (Yr Wyddfa).*

Start: *There is a moderate sized car park at Pen-y-Pass (often full early during the summer). A fee is payable. Grid ref: SH 647 557. Alternatively, use the Park and Ride at Nant Peris. Grid ref: SH 607 583.*

FEW WOULD BEGRUDGE CWM DYLI'S CLAIM to being Snowdon's most impressive and dramatic valley. But it is also the mountain's best known and has been painted and photographed since the first visitors began to come to Snowdonia almost two centuries ago. The cwm is enclosed by the rocky arms of the famous 'Snowdon Horseshoe' producing one of the most appealing mountain views in Britain. The grand scenery is enhanced by two mountain lakes, the upper lake—Glaslyn—is cradled in an impressive rock basin with the summit cone rising almost 500 metres (about 1,600 feet) above its blue-green waters.

Sadly, Cwm Dyli has also been despoiled since the mid-nineteenth century by mining activities, but it remains one of the finest approaches to the mountain.

The route: From the Pen-y-Pass car park the obvious exit from the lower car park is the Miners' Track, the Pyg Track exits from the higher car park just behind the café ('Gorphwysfa Restaurant') through a gap in the stone wall and under power lines. A well constructed path—with views down the Llanberis Pass—leads to Bwlch Moch, the point at which you enter the Snowdon Horseshoe. From here there are views

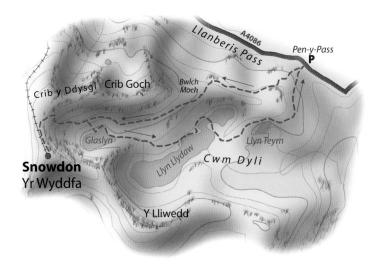

down to Llyn Llydaw and it's causeway, and beyond to the 300m face of Y Lliwedd. Ahead is Snowdon looking deceptively close.

To the right at this point is the steep path leading up to Crib Goch, but the Pyg Track continues over the stiles ahead to contour along the mountain's southern slopes.

Following the Pyg Track you eventually reach a superb viewpoint where Glaslyn and the dramatic summit cone of Snowdon can be seen to perfection rising above the lake.

Continue on the contouring path to an even closer viewpoint directly above Glaslyn. From here the path curves around the cwm passing the junction with the Miners' Track (marked by an upright stone—take note of this for the descent) coming up from the left and the remains of the copper mines. Higher up you reach the foot of the famous 'Zig-zags' which negotiate the final steep slopes to Bwlch Glas. The bwlch is marked by a 2-metre upright stone pillar and it is here you meet with the Llanberis Path and the Snowdon Mountain Railway. Turn left for the final ten minute walk to the summit.

Yr Wyddfa, the summit of Snowdon, from the Pyg Track

Looking down into Cwm Dyli from the Zig-zags to Glaslyn and Llyn Llydaw

To descend, return to the upright stone on Bwlch Glas and descend the 'Zig-zags'. As the angle eases the path swings leftwards taking a more gradual traversing line with mining remains below. Look for the junction with the Miners' Track noted on the ascent and marked by an upright stone pillar. This path descends directly down a wide scree gully to the shore of Glaslyn. (Avoid a path which breaks away slightly earlier and takes a more diagonal line passing close to mines before reaching the lake.)

Follow the path along the shore of the lake to the outflow, then descend beside the stream to the shores of Llyn Llydaw. Continue along the northern shore of the lake and across the stone causeway originally built by miners working in the Glaslyn Mines during the nineteenth century. Beyond the causeway the path is virtually level and wide—almost a road—and contours the slopes back to Pen-y-Pass.

Looking into Cwm Dyli from Crib y Ddysgl

21. *The Snowdon Horseshoe*

Outline: **SCRAMBLE** *This magnificent route provides moderate, exposed scrambling for much of its length with one or two sections where a fall could be serious. The most demanding section will be found on the Crib Goch Pinnacles with the return leg over Y Lliwedd offering grand views from the top of the largest precipice in Wales. This section involves rough, rocky walking rather than the type of scrambling encountered on Crib Goch.*

Distance: *11.5km/7¼ miles.*

Height gained: *1,180m/3,850ft.*

Summits: *Crib Goch, Crib y Ddysgl, Snowdon & Y Lliwedd.*

Start: *There is a moderate sized car park at Pen-y-Pass (often full early during the summer). A fee is payable. Grid ref: SH 647 557. Alternatively, use the Park and Ride located at Nant Peris. Grid ref: SH 607 583.*

THE SNOWDON HORSESHOE OFFERS A MAGNIFICENT MOUNTAIN DAY—possibly the best scramble south of the Scottish Highlands. It follows the skyline of Cwm Dyli formed by the two great eastern ridges of Y Lliwedd and the infamous Crib Goch.

The cautionary note in the outline paragraph should be noted by anyone unsure of their ability in situations of exposed scrambling. Crib Goch is a rock peak and you can not reach its summit without scrambling, although the standard is not high and should be within the ability of most individuals. Under ice and snow this route becomes a low-end winter climb and should be treated as such.

The route: Take the Pyg Track, a well constructed path—with views down the Llanberis Pass—to Bwlch Moch, the point at which you enter the Snowdon Horseshoe. The obvious exit from the lower car park is the Miners' Track, the Pyg Track exits from the higher car park just behind the café ('Gorphwysfa Restaurant') through a gap in the stone wall and beneath power lines.

From here there are views down to Llyn Llydaw and it's causeway, and beyond to the 300m face of Y Lliwedd. Ahead is Snowdon looking

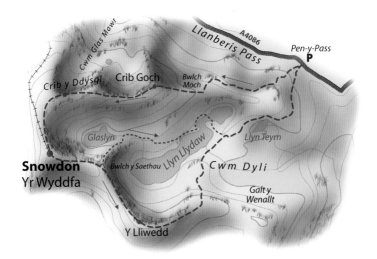

deceptively close. Here the path forks. The Pyg Track continues over stiles ahead to contour the southern slopes of Crib Goch, whilst the Crib Goch path bears right up over the shoulder. The path has been surfaced with large stone slabs making it almost impossible to miss.

Higher up your way is barred by the large rock step guarding the East Ridge. The left-hand side of this step is both steep and hard, while the right-hand side eventually merges into the shattered east face of the mountain. The most frequented line is almost direct, a little left of centre and involves moderate rock scrambling up a series of grooves and corners. Once above the rock step the easier rocks of the upper East Ridge lead spectacularly to the summit.

This is one of the most dramatic places in Snowdonia and if you can relax it is a good place to rest and enjoy the fantastic scenery that surrounds you. The knife edge of the North Ridge sweeps down into the Llanberis Pass to the right, but it is likely to be the narrow ridge ahead which will grab your attention. The views are magnificent.

The ridge is very narrow, almost level and exposed for about 300m. It is usual on this section to drop down a metre or so on the left side

Traversing the narrow crest of Crib Goch

Crib Goch seen in profile from the north

of the ridge and use the crest for hand holds which will also give you a little protection from the exposure on the north side.

The ridge eventually leads to the first of the famous 'Pinnacles'. These can be tackled direct or more usually turned on the left by an obvious traversing path, but be careful not to descend too far. From the gap before the final pinnacle there is a short exposed scramble on the north side overlooking a gully and requiring care, but once over this section the descent to Bwlch Coch is straightforward. The major difficulties are now behind you.

The ridge is now much wider, far less exposed and rises to one last rock step on the approach to Crib y Ddysgl. A short narrow section just before the summit is normally turned on the right.

From Crib y Ddysgl follow the edge of Cwm Dyli to Bwlch Glas (marked by a 2-metre upright stone) where you join the Llanberis Path and the routes coming up the 'Zig-zags' from Glaslyn. A short easy walk of about ten minutes will take you to the summit.

Approaching the Crib Goch Pinnacles with Snowdon behind

If you enjoy crowds, the new summit visitor centre is the place to lunch, otherwise you will want to be on your way. Descend the upper section of the Watkin Path which starts on the South Ridge and, like Bwlch Glas, is marked by a 2-metre upright stone. The path crosses the south face of the mountain diagonally to Bwlch y Saethau.

(Here you can cut the route short if needed by scrambling down Y Gribin—a moderate rock ridge which drops to Glaslyn. The standard is a little easier than Crib Goch, technically harder than continuing over Y Lliwedd, but easier on tired knees. The main problem in descent, as with all such routes, is locating the top of the ridge. In good visibility you will know that you are in the correct location as the entire ridge is visible below. In poor visibility the route is best avoided without prior knowledge.

For Y Gribin bear left at Bwlch y Saethau to the edge of the cwm above Glaslyn. There is a small pool amongst the grass and rocks here—not the only one unfortunately—with a narrow but visible path leading diagonally down to the start of the ridge. This point is marked by a small cairn.

As already mentioned in clear conditions you will see the ridge below you curving down to the outflow of Glaslyn. The best line keeps to the crest and avoids both the extreme right-hand side where the cliffs fall alarmingly to Llyn Llydaw and the left where the scrambling is poor. Turn right along the Miners' Track, down to Llyn Llydaw and cross the causeway back to Pen-y-Pass.)

To continue over Y Lliwedd from Bwlch y Saethau, follow the Watkin Path down to Bwlch Ciliau where it turns right at a junction down into Cwm Llan. Keep ahead here on the path which follows the edge of the cliffs to Y Lliwedd which can be seen rising dramatically ahead.

At the top of the ridge, continue over the twin summits of Y Lliwedd and follow the good path down to a cairn marking the exit from the ridge. From here drop down into Cwm Dyli to the outflow of Llyn Llydaw where you join the Miners' Track. Turn right and follow the Miners' Track back to Pen-y-Pass.

The twin summits of Y Lliwedd with Snowdon (Yr Wyddfa) behind

Snowdon (Yr Wyddfa) from the south

22. Snowdon from the south— Cwm Llan Horseshoe

Outline: *A beautiful approach through woods to a remote hanging valley is followed by a spectacular ridge walk. The final rise to Snowdon is over steep scree, but is more than compensated for by the easy jaunt down the South Ridge with its spectacular views and the option to include the shapely summit of Yr Aran.*

Distance: *16km/10 miles.*

Height gained: *1,640m/5,380ft.*

Summits: *Y Lliwedd, Snowdon (Yr Wyddfa) & Yr Aran.*

Starting point: *Pont Bethania car park near Nantgwynant on the A498, about 3.5km/2¼ miles east of Beddgelert. Grid ref: SH 628 506.*

THE MAIN ATTRACTION OF THIS ROUTE is the beautiful approach through woods and beside the cascading Afon Cwm Llan to the remote hanging valley of Cwm Merch and the superb viewpoint of Gallt y Wenallt. The traverse of Y Lliwedd is spectacular, passing along the edge of the highest precipice in Wales.

The descent from Snowdon by the South Ridge has the advantage of being slightly off the normal 'trade routes' and thus less crowded. It is also a fine ridge, particularly in the upper half where it narrows to form the famous 'Saddle' at Bwlch Main. If you still have the energy, Yr Aran makes a fine finish for the day.

The route: Turn left out of the car park, cross the bridge and in about 100m or so turn right into a narrow lane. Don't follow the lane which leads to the farms of Hafod-y-llan, instead, go up stone steps immediately ahead, signed for the 'Watkin Path'. This new section of path weaves through mature woods above the lane to eventually join the old route—now a rough track—with a view out over the valley. Go left through the gate (signed 'Watkin') and follow the rising track, soon with the cascading Afon Cwm Llan down to your right. The path soon swings left with a view ahead to waterfalls and the remains of an old incline rising steeply up the hillside. Continue along the path, crossing the incline and a little further on, immediately before a gate,

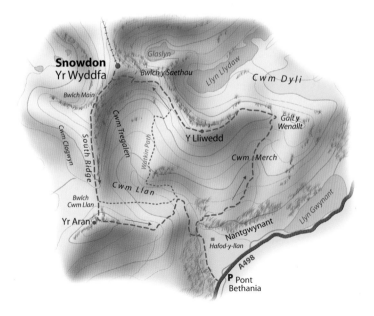

On the summit of Gallt y Wenallt with Snowdon and Crib Goch behind

turn right and walk beside the wall down to an old stone slab bridge over the stream.

Cross the bridge and go ahead up the bank ignoring a stile and gate to the left. A little higher up, a second stile by a gate leads onto an old mining road—now a pleasant green track—which leads through oak woods and scattered pines. This section is a delight. All too soon the trees thin out and after a stile by a gate in the wall disappear altogether. The path continues to climb, eventually zig-zaging up to a gateway in a wall. Go through the gateway and follow the path as it turns sharp left, then sharp right.

The path climbs gently for a while, then levels to contour beside an old wall, eventually bringing you to abandoned mines in the broad shallow hanging valley of Cwm Merch. Just before the ruins, take a narrow footpath which bears left off the main path (if you reach the mine buildings you have gone too far). This very soon becomes vague, so scramble up left for a few metres over a rocky stream to a level area beside a ruin. Bear right above the ruin and pick up a path which crosses

Looking down from the summit of Y Lliwedd to Llyn Llydaw

the rust-coloured spoil from the workings above. Continue ahead now on a vague, grassy path to the bwlch on the skyline.

The minor top of Gallt y Wenallt lies to the right—worth the short detour for the stunning view—otherwise turn left on the path which hugs the edge of the cliffs rising above Cwm Dyli. The steepening path is easily followed now to Y Lliwedd's twin summits, perched impressively above a 300m face—the largest cliff face in Wales.

From here the descent along the ridge is obvious to Bwlch Cilau where the Watkin Path joins from the left (a possible return if time is short). Follow the path ahead to Bwlch y Saethau ('pass of the arrows')—a name associating the place with King Arthur—before the final steep rise to Snowdon.

At the time of writing the path is quite eroded and negotiates the steep scree-covered southern face of the mountain to join the South Ridge at an upright stone just below the summit which lies up to the right.

From the summit return along the South Ridge passing the upright stone again. A little further on it narrows considerably at the famous Bwlch Main, better known as 'The Saddle'. The ridge is interesting here rather than spectacular and there are fine airy views into both Cwm Clogwyn on the right and Cwm Tregalen to the left with a moderate amount of exposure. After Bwlch Main there is a short rise to a subsidiary top then an enjoyable easy descent to Bwlch Cwm Llan, the pass which separates the South Ridge from Yr Aran, Snowdon's shapely southern satellite.

On the South Ridge near Bwlch Main

On the lower section of the South Ridge with Yr Aran behind

(The easiest and shortest option from here is to turn left and follow the path down to, and then along the course of an old tramway until you are above the ruins of Plas Cwm Llan were a path heads steeply down to join the Watkin Path at its exit from Cwm Llan. Turn right and follow the Watkin Path back to Pont Bethania.)

To include Yr Aran, take the path ahead up beside the wall. Stay by the wall until you reach the east ridge where the wall turns left along the grassy crest. Turn right here for the summit.

Retrace your steps back down to the wall and follow it (on the left-hand side) east along the ridge. About 100m before the wall turns south (right), almost at the ridge end (GR. 614 515), take a path on the left which descends diagonally, passing old mine workings on the right. Head down northeast over rough ground to reach an old tramway near GR. 619 519. Depending on where you joined the tramway (ideally just after it has crossed the stream and where it is supported on one side by stonework) you may have to turn left, right, or go straight across on a path which descends to join the Watkin Path. Turn right and follow the Watkin Path back to Pont Bethania.

Looking into upper Cwm Glas (Cwm Uchaf) from the top of the Gyrn Lâs Ridge

23. Cwm Glas Horseshoe— Crib Goch/Gyrn Lâs Ridge

Outline: SCRAMBLE *After a steep walk into the wilds of Cwm Glas Mawr easy scrambling in a rocky stream-bed leads to a fine narrow rock arête and finally Crib Goch's airy summit. The famous traverse of the Crib Goch/Crib y Ddysgl ridge is followed by a descent of the little known Gyrn Lâs Ridge which gives a few pitches of easy scrambling in the upper section.*

Distance: *9km/5½ miles.*

Height gained: *1,150m/3,750ft.*

Summits: *Crib Goch & Crib y Ddysgl.*

Starting point: *Blaen-y-Nant in the Llanberis Pass on the A4086 (grid ref: SH 623 570). Parking could be a problem. If the lay-bys are full (likely during the summer) park at Nant Peris and take the Park and Ride. Grid ref: SH 607 583.*

THIS ROUTE WILL BE FAVOURED BY THOSE WHO ENJOY SOLITUDE. The wild, rugged beauty of Cwm Glas Mawr and Cwm Uchaf is seen to perfection from their enclosing arms which also provide excellent scrambling. Only along the Crib Goch/Crib y Ddysgl ridge are you likely to meet other scramblers.

This route uses the best sections of the more famous Snowdon Horseshoe, with an ascent of the less frequented North Ridge of Crib Goch and a descent of the almost unknown Gyrn Lâs Ridge. Views into the secluded Cwm Glas Mawr and Cwm Uchaf are stunning both in ascent and descent. In grade it is similar to the Snowdon Horseshoe reaching its crux on the traverse of Crib Goch's Pinnacle Ridge. Read the cautionary note in route 21 and don't attempt this route if you are unsure of your ability in situations of exposed scrambling.

The main problem with this circuit is a suitable approach to Crib Goch's North Ridge. The lower section of the ridge has been sliced off to form the fine, clean face of Dinas Mot—rock climbing rather than scrambling territory. Traditionally the North Ridge has been approached either from Pen-y-Pass via the Pyg Track, or from Cwm

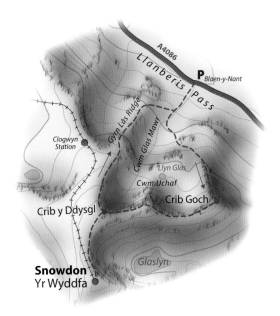

Crib Goch from the northeast showing the North Ridge on the right-hand skyline

Uchaf, but neither of these options give a satisfying 'horseshoe' round and they are both now little used and indistinct on the ground. This route uses a stream-carved weakness in the crags to provide an easy scramble and a complete contrast to the airy arêtes above. A dry spell is needed for the stream section which should not be attempted in winter conditions.

The route: Cross the bridge at Blaen-y-Nant, go over the stile ahead and cross another wooden bridge on the right. Turn sharp left here and walk directly uphill beside the stream. After a gap in the upper wall, the path becomes clearer as it leads up into Cwm Glas Mawr.

In about 150m bear left on a faint path which soon disappears. Cross the stream and aim for the large crag with a dark, wet face (Craig y Rhaeadr) partly visible ahead. As you enter Cwm Glas Mawr the entire face becomes visible. To the left of this, a stream can be seen cascading from the upper cwm into a small gully. Aim for the base of this gully.

As you approach the stream, keep to its right-hand side and rise to the first of the rocks—a broken grey rib. Climb this to a point level with a small waterfall. The rock rib above this is much harder but can be turned by a short grove a few metres to the right. Easy ground through heather on a faint path follows. Soon a scree path becomes visible on the far side of the stream—a little higher up move left to a rock which overlooks the stream above the highest waterfall. Below and to the right there is a small pool with a cascade above. Climb down to the pool by some short rock steps and cross the stream. Immediately to the left of the cascade there is a broken rib which provides good easy scrambling, but only in dry conditions. Alternatively, use the scree path immediately to the left. Above this the stream can be scrambled in most conditions.

Higher up the stream forks—keep straight ahead (left fork) to where another easy broken rib to the right of the stream gives more low-grade scrambling.

Emerge in a wide grass bay lined with slabby rounded rocks. The impressive nose of Clogwyn y Person is partly visible over to the right and there is a boulder perched on the slabs ahead. Bear left up to the skyline now which marks the start of Crib Goch's North Ridge.

The ridge is rounded and grassy at first but soon steepens into a zig-zag path up red scree to what appears to be a subsidiary top. This is steep, hard work but soon the ridge narrows and things become much easier and more interesting.

Snowdon from Glyder Fach showing the North Ridge of Crib Goch and the Crib y Ddysgl ridge with Snowdon behind

(If conditions are not dry enough for the stream scramble, the North Ridge can be approached via Cwm Glas Mawr and Cwm Uchaf as follows: Take the described route from Blaean-y-Nant to the gap in the wall but don't bear left after 150m, instead, continue on the path ahead. As you enter the cwm the angle eases and there are two large boulders which the path passes between. Cross the stream a little further on and head across the broad flat base of the cwm towards the imposing headwall. The path into the upper cwm begins at the left-hand side of this headwall where a stream cascades over the broken rocks.

Head left up the scree path which reaches the lip of the cwm below the prowlike nose of Clogwyn y Person. A little to the left is Llyn Glas—a beautiful mountain pool with a tiny island and solitary tree. Pass the lake and head towards Crib Goch's North Ridge on the skyline.)

Although it is quite narrow, the shattered, loose sides of the ridge mean that the crest provides the easiest line. There is increasing exposure, particularly down the east face to the left, but only in the final few metres to it its junction with the East Ridge is there any technical scrambling.

Crib Goch is a true mountain summit—a narrow rock peak with stunning views and dizzying exposure on almost every side. If you thrive

The Gyrn Lâs Ridge seen from the Llanberis Pass

in this environment you'll love it, if not you'll hate it and you shouldn't really be here! If you can relax and take in the view it is one of the most unique spots in Snowdonia.

The route continues along the narrow west ridge to the famous Pinnacles which provide the crux as far as difficulty and exposure are concerned. The ridge is very narrow, almost level and exposed for about 300m. The usual technique on this section is to drop down a metre or so on the left side and use the crest for hand holds. This will also give you a little protection from the exposure on the north side.

The 'Pinnacles' can be tackled direct, or more usually turned on the left by an obvious traversing path, but be careful not to descend too far. The traversing path leads to a gap before the final pinnacle where a short exposed section on the north side overlooking a gully requires care (crux). Once over this section the descent to the welcoming grass of Bwlch Coch is straightforward. The major difficulties are now over.

The ridge is now much wider, far less exposed and rises to one last rock step on the approach to Crib y Ddysgl. A short narrow section just before the summit can be turned on the right. *(Snowdon summit is an easy jaunt across Bwlch Glas, but you will need to return to this summit to continue.)* From Crib y Ddysgl follow the edge of the cwm almost due north to the top of the Gyrn Lâs Ridge.

The start of the ridge is quite easy to locate even in poor visibility and begins with simple scrambling in a short gully. This is followed by a short section on the rocky crest of the ridge to a grass shoulder. Below this there is another section of scrambling, slightly harder this time, to reach a much larger grass shoulder. These scrambling pitches can all be avoided by easier ground to the left if needed.

The ridge is still steep but the rocks are gone now and you will be able to keep your hands in your pockets for most of the way.

A faint path is beginning to establish itself, but at the time of writing this does not help you to decide where to exit the ridge. The best place is approximately level with the large crag with the brown water stain down its middle passed at the start of the walk. At this point bear right to join the Cwm Glas Mawr path beside the stream which can be seen below. Turn left down the path to return to Blaen-y-Nant.

Moel Cynghorion and Moel Eilio in the distance

24. Moel Eilio group

Outline: *A rising lane leads from Llanberis onto the broad open moors above the town. This is followed by the easy-angled northeast ridge to the summit of Moel Eilio. The connecting ridge to Foel Gron and Foel Goch is a switchback grassy ridge with a return to Llanberis by old farm roads.*

Distance: *12km/8 miles.*

Height gained: *790m/2,560ft.*

Summits: *Moel Eilio, Foel Gron & Foel Goch.*

Starting point: *There is plenty of parking space opposite the Railway Station in Llanberis, but during the high season the car parks get very crowded, so you need to get there fairly early. Grid ref: SH 582 599.*

THESE HILLS SUFFER FROM THE PROXIMITY of their larger and more famous neighbour. As a result they are overlooked by the majority who only have eyes for Snowdon. However, they provide an excellent ridge walk with superb views, particularly of Snowdon and are often clear when the higher peaks wear a cap of cloud.

The route: From the centre of Llanberis follow 'Ffordd Capel Coch', a lane signed for the Youth Hostel. Pass the Youth Hostel on the left and carry on past the farmhouse called 'Hafod Lydan'. Where the road turns left immediately after the house 'Hafod Uchaf' on the left, turn right along a track. Go through the gate or over the stile and continue until you are about 50m from the wall and stile ahead. Turn left onto a path which rises to a gate and stile in the wall.

Go through the gate and continue along the path until the lake comes into view. Turn right up steep grass (no path) to the crest of the ridge. Once on the rounded crest, turn left and walk beside the fence. There are faint footpaths on both sides of the fence and stiles over any crossing fences. Near the summit join the broad path which

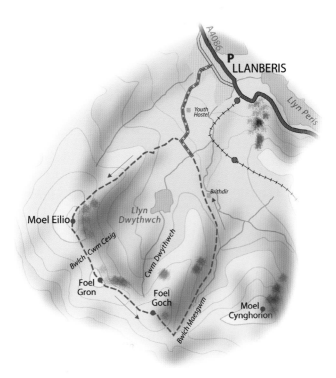

Looking along the ridge to Snowdon

rises up the flat northern flanks of the mountain. The summit at 726m (2,380ft) is marked by a circular drystone shelter.

The ridge continues southeast to Bwlch Cwm Cesig with Cwm Dwythwch and Llyn Dwythwch down below to your left. From the bwlch climb to Foel Gron (629m) and Foel Goch beyond at 605m.

Return to Llanberis can be made either by the broad grass ridge to the north or a steep grass descent southeast which will bring you down to Bwlch Maesgwm, between Foel Goch and Moel Cynghorion. *(Moel Cynghorion can easily be included by an out-and-back walk up the grass ridge ahead.)*

From the bwlch turn left (north) onto a path (thought to be an ancient packhorse trail) and follow this for 3km/1¾ miles passing the farmhouse of 'Brithdir' to the lane used at the start of the walk ('Ffordd Capel Coch'). Turn right and follow the lane back to Llanberis.

The east ridge of Craig Cwm Silyn

The Eifionydd hills

The hills of the Nantlle Ridge from Mynydd Mawr

Eifionydd hills

THE EIFIONYDD HILLS SUFFER FROM the fame and stature of nearby Snowdon which towers above them across the divide of Nant Colwyn. From this lofty summit most eyes are drawn north and eastwards across the wilds of Cwm Dyli to the Glyder and the distant Carneddau, or east to the wedge of Moel Siabod. Westwards, it is the glistening sea which grabs the attention—the distant curve of Cardigan Bay, the coastline of Lleyn emerging from the haze, or the plains of Anglesey spread out like a map. The handful of foreground hills, often silhouetted by an afternoon sun, are barely noticed and frequently dismissed. Being little more than two-thirds its height, they are grassier, less rocky and generally less dramatic than Snowdon and its neighbours—'fells' rather than mountains. But this does have a flip side—they are not nearly so busy. No need to dodge the crowds here, much of the time you will have the hills to yourself.

The range is not so easily defined as the previous groups. Most of

the summits lie in a great horseshoe enclosing the hidden valley of Cwm Pennant. Just one lies away from this main ridge—the isolated Mynydd Mawr. The eastern arm of the horseshoe consists of Moel Hebog and one or two lesser summits which straddle the undulating ridge running north above the Beddgelert Forest. The western arm forms the striking Nantlle Ridge, its traverse offering one of the best ridge walks of its kind in Wales.

Despite the number of summits in this group, there are surprisingly few recognised routes. Moel Hebog, the highest, is usually ascended on its own from Beddgelert with a return made by the same route, but the neighbouring tops to the north are well worth including. A better option is to follow the ridge north from Moel Hebog, with a return to Beddgelert through the Beddgelert Forest.

The hills of the Nantlle Ridge need little introduction being one of Snowdonia's best ridge walks. The normal approach starts from the village of Rhyd-Ddu. The main problem here is that there is no convenient way of turning it into a circular route. Logically this is a

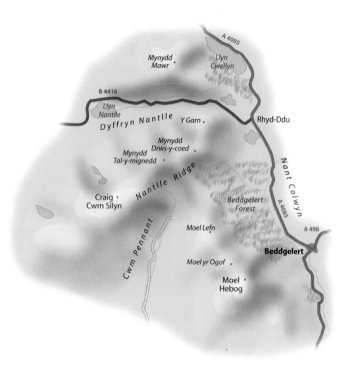

linear walk, starting at Rhyd-Ddu and finishing at the village of Nebo at its western end. If you can arrange transport at both ends, this is the best option. Alternatively, you can return by dropping into the head of Cwm Pennant from Craig Cwm Silyn and crossing the bwlch into the northern edge of the Beddgelert Forest.

Despite its modest height, Mynydd Mawr is a prominent summit in the group, due mainly to the fact that it is separated by deeply-cut valleys on all sides. The ascent from the hamlet of Rhyd-Ddu provides a fine approach on a sweeping grass edge with views across the tottering towers of Craig y Bera and down to the beautiful Llyn Cwellyn.

Y Garn and the ridge of Mynydd Drws-y-coed from Dyffryn Nantlle

Looking across Dyffryn Nantlle to the Nantlle Ridge from Mynydd Mawr

25. Mynydd Mawr from Rhyd-Ddu

Outline: *Easy walking on forest tracks, then a sweeping grass ridge to Foel Rudd and Mynydd Mawr. Descent is made by Afon Goch, rocky in its lower section, to the shores of Llyn Cwellyn, with a return along forest tracks.*

Distance: *10.5km/6½ miles.*

Height gained: *761m/2,500ft.*

Summits: *Foel Rudd & Mynydd Mawr.*

Starting point: *The village of Rhyd-Ddu on the A4085 Caernarfon to Beddgelert road. There are paying car parks for Snowdon immediately south of the village. Grid ref: SH 571 525.*

THE MAIN APPEAL OF THIS MINIATURE MOUNTAIN is the stunning views to be enjoyed across the gulf of Dyffryn Nantlle. A superb mini-mountain day (or half-day for the seasoned mountain walker), with wide views.

The route: From the 'Cwellyn Arms' in the centre of Rhyd-Ddu (junction of the A4085 and B4418) take the B4418 Nantlle road. In about 150m turn right onto a forest road immediately after 'Cefn Cwellyn'. Follow the forest road for just over 1km/¾ mile before bearing left on a signed footpath which climbs to a stile on the edge of the woods.

Cross the stile and turn right along the forest edge which follows the crest of the ridge. At the end of the trees, climb the steepening grass ridge ahead to gain the subsidiary summit of Foel Rudd.

Follow the easy-angled connecting ridge westwards from Foel Rudd passing along the crest of Craig y Bera with dramatic views down the shattered crags to the pastures of Nantlle below. Soon the path veers rightwards away from the cliffs to make an easy rise to the rounded summit with its superb views to Snowdon and south to the famous Nantlle Ridge.

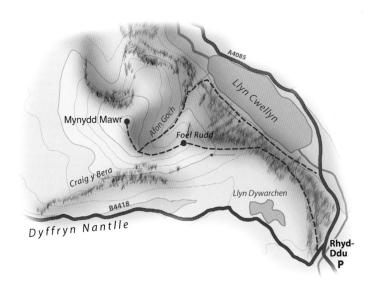

Return can be made via the ascent route, but a more interesting circular walk with more of an exploratory feel can be made by returning to the crest of Craig y Bera, then bearing left down easy angled but initially pathless heather slopes with occasional scree, to join a faint path on the left bank of a stream (Afon Goch). Lower down just before the angle steepens and you can see Llyn Cwellyn below, cross over to the right bank of the stream. This avoids difficult ground where the stream cascades into a small ravine beneath the dark dripping crags of Castell Cidwm *('Castle of the Wolf')*.

Below the ravine and waterfall, and just before woods, cross the stream again. Make your way between rocks and young pines to cross a stone wall in the corner by a rock face on the left. Walk down to the shore of the lake.

Just before the water turn right on a path to a gate which continues to pass a small quarry on the right. Soon, join a forest track and follow it to the road (A4085). Turn right and follow the road back to Rhyd-Ddu.

On the summit of Mynydd Mawr with the Nantlle Ridge behind

Moel Hebog rising above the Beddgelert Forest

26. Moel Hebog from Beddgelert

Outline: *A steep, direct ascent of Moel Hebog's northeast ridge is followed by an elevated walk along the broad switchback ridge connecting it to the minor summits of Moel yr Ogof and Moel Lefn. Return is made by the forest paths and tracks of the Beddgelert Forest.*

Distance: *12km/7½ miles.*

Height gained: *995m/3,260ft.*

Summits: *Moel Hebog, Moel yr Ogof & Moel Lefn.*

Starting point: *The village of Beddgelert. Car parks fill early in the summer season. Begin the walk at the 'Royal Goat Hotel'.*
Grid ref: SH 588 480.

ANY MOUNTAIN STANDING IN Snowdon's shadow should be completely overwhelmed by it—not so Moel Hebog. Rising immediately to the west of Beddgelert and with Snowdon safely out of sight behind Yr Aran, it completely dominates the village. It is seen at its best on the descent from Rhyd-Ddu to Beddgelert against a foreground of conifers and lakes.

This route takes the usual direct ascent from Beddgelert and then continues north along the rounded ridge and the smaller summits of Moel Ogof and Moel Lefn, with a return through the woods of the Beddgelert Forest.

The route: Turn right by the 'Royal Goat Hotel' into an access road and where this bends left behind the hotel turn right onto a path which passes behind houses. Ignore the signed footpath to the left continuing ahead to walk beside the Welsh Highland Railway. The path soon drops to pass under the railway by a bridge. Turn right after the bridge and at a T junction with an access road, turn left. Follow the road crossing the railway twice to the farmhouse of 'Cwm Cloch Canol'.

Turn right through a gate opposite the farmhouse and follow the well defined footpath across an area of rough open pasture. Soon the path steepens and rises to a stile and gate in the wall which leads onto the northeast ridge. Ascend the ridge on a steep, direct path until the angle eases as you approach the crags at the head of the impressive Cwm Bleiddlaid.

From here the path bends left to avoid the crags, then turns right-wards up the scree-covered upper slopes of the mountain (a section of easy scrambling to the right can be used to avoid this scree) to a

Snowdon from Moel Ogof

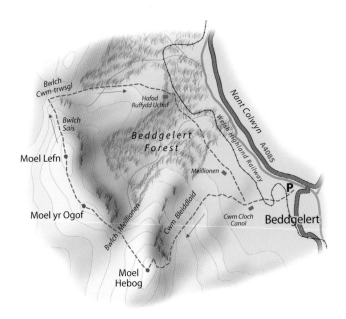

subsidiary top at the head of the crags. The highest point is an easy, short walk to the south.

From the summit descend northwest beside the wall to Bwlch Meillionen. From here ascend directly through a cleft in the crags above passing an area of pools to reach the next summit—Moel yr Ogof ('hill of the cave', said to have once been the hideout of Owain Glyndŵr).

Continue northwest to the next top, Moel Lefn, a straightforward 1km/¾ mile walk along the rounded ridge crossing a fence partway at its junction with an old stone wall.

From Moel Lefn continue north over grass, then descend steeply to a small bwlch—Bwlch Sais, *(Englishman's pass)*. The path continues the descent to pass a tiny quarry on the right with a wall ahead. Cross the fence where it joins the wall and follow the path left down beside the wall to a larger bwlch—Bwlch Cwm-trwsgl (GR. 553 496).

A stile on the right here leads into the woods of the Beddgelert Forest. Now for the complicated route finding! Cross the stile and enter the trees. Descend a rocky and often wet path to a forest road. Turn left here and after 100m or so, look for a narrow, but well-used footpath on the right. Follow this path through the trees keeping right at a fork to enter a clearing by a gap in the wall. Follow the obvious traversing path (marked by well spaced blue posts) straight ahead with superb views to Snowdon. A second path develops on the left as you cross the clearing—ignore this path.

A stile in the fence ahead takes you back into the woods again. Follow the path to a forest road, turn left, then after a few metres turn right onto a narrow footpath which takes you directly down the hillside crossing a number of forest roads again. Keep descending until you cross over a wall into a small rough field with a house ('Hafod Ruffydd Uchaf') on the right. Walk down the field edge passing the cottage to a stile which leads onto a forest road.

Turn right along the forest road. Ignore tracks off to the right and in 350m, immediately after the forest road bends left and just before it runs beside the Welsh Highland Railway, take a surfaced path on the right which soon crosses the river by an old stone bridge. Just after the bridge go through a gate on the right into fields. Walk along the left edge of the field beside the woods to enter a section of enclosed path between the field and the woods. At the end of this and the end of the woods bear left down to an access road.

Turn right up the road towards the farmhouse of 'Meillionen'. Pass the front of the house to go through a small gateway in the wall. Head diagonally-left through the following field to the far left-hand corner where stone steps lead over the wall into the woods again. Take the path half-left through the trees to reach a forest road. Turn right up this and just before a sharp right-hand bend take the signed path on the left. Cross the stream by two gates and follow the well-used path ahead beside the wall. This path is well-used and easily followed and leads back to the farmhouse of 'Cwm Cloch Canol'. Turn left down the access road and retrace the outward route back to Beddgelert.

Trum y Ddysgl from the shoulder of Craig Cwm Silyn

27. *The Nantlle Ridge*

Outline: *After a short, steep climb to gain the first peak, the ridge is pure delight. There are one or two sections with easy scrambling on Mynydd Drws-y-coed, but the most of the ridge is rounded and grassy with wide views to Lleyn, the sea and back to Snowdon.*

Distance: *14km/8¾ miles.*

Height gained: *1,200m/3,900ft.*

Summits: *Y Garn, Mynydd Drws-y-coed, Trum y Ddysgl, Mynydd Tal-y-mignedd & Craig Cwm Silyn.*

Starting point: *The village of Rhyd-Ddu on the A4085 Caernarfon to Beddgelert road. There are car parks for Snowdon immediately south of the village. Grid ref: SH 571 526.*

THE WALL OF HILLS WHICH RISE TO THE SOUTH of Nantlle are linked conveniently by a graceful sweeping ridge which provides one of Snowdonia's finest mountain walks. Only two points on the ridge exceed 700 metres, but what these hills lack in height they certainly make up for in their rugged and often dramatic outlines.

The approach to Mynydd Tal-y-mignedd with Craig Cwm Silyn in the distance

As a mountain ridge walk, the Nantlle Ridge can probably only be bettered by the ridges of Snowdon. But there is a problem. Although all the summits are connected with minimum loss of height, it is hard to make a satisfying circular walk. The options are: to walk it as a linear route and arrange transport at both ends; walk it in both directions; retrace your steps to the central summit of Trum y Ddysgl, descending the south ridge to Bwlch-y-Ddwy-elor and then return through Beddgelert Forest; descend into the head of Cwm Pennant from Bwlch Dros-bern and then head for Bwlch-y-Ddwy-elor avoiding the ascents back along the ridge, but much of the terrain is pathless.

The route: Opposite the car park entrance a kissing gate leads onto a footpath paved with flat stones which crosses a damp flat field with the dramatic profile of Y Garn, the northeastern terminus of the Nantlle Ridge, directly ahead. At a stream bear left to a footbridge with a stone cottage on the right. Cross the driveway and shortly join it again a little further on continuing to the road (B4418).

Don't go onto the road, instead, take the signed footpath on the left which initially passes along field edges with the dramatic outlines of Y Garn and Mynydd Drws-y-coed rising ahead. After a stream the path curves right and begins the steep climb to the first summit—Y Garn. After a large rock with white arrows painted on it the path divides. Ignore the path ahead which continues through the forest to Bwlch-y-Ddwy-elor and Cwm Pennant (used as one of the return options), instead, bear right rising steeply and directly up the eastern slopes of Y Garn.

After a long, stiff pull the angle begins to ease and just before the highest point a well-built stone wall is cross by a ladder stile. The summit cairn lies a few metres to the northwest perched on the very edge of the cliffs falling into Dyffryn Nantlle (take care in poor visibility).

The view from here and throughout the walk is extensive taking in the western slopes of Snowdon and the dramatic southern face of Mynydd Mawr which dominates the opposite side of Dyffryn Nantlle. However, your eye is most likely to be drawn by the imposing profile rising along

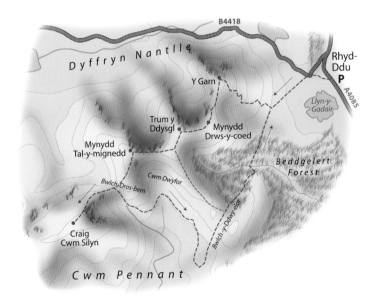

the ridge to the south. Mynydd Drws-y-coed is often seen as a hazy silhouette against the midday sun and can look quite intimidating but don't despair, the ridge presents little more than a brief, enjoyable (and avoidable) scramble.

The path heads south, soon beside the wall crossed near the summit. Stay by the wall as the ridge narrows and soon you begin to use your hands here and there. The climax of the scrambling comes in the short final rise to Mynydd Drws-y-coed. There is exposure here but only on the right-hand side of the ridge. If big drops are not your thing keep to the left where alternative lines avoid both exposure and scrambling.

All too soon (or thankfully, depending on your viewpoint) the scrambling is over and the ridge continues as a fine narrow grass edge. After a short descent to the bwlch the ridge rises impressively to Trum y Ddysgl. The best option is along the ridge crest but a slightly easier line forks left just above the bwlch to emerge at the mountain's western top. *(From this point note the south ridge—a broad grassy arm which descends steeply to Bwlch-y-Ddwy-elor and can be used as a return to Rhyd-Ddu).*

Looking along the ridge to Trum y Ddysgl with Snowdon in the distance

Mynydd Tal-y-mignedd from the descent into Cwm Pennant

If you stayed with the ridge crest you will arrive at the eastern top where you get a fine view back along the ridge with Snowdon in the distance. From Trum y Ddysgl the ridge continues due west narrowing at one point almost enough to require a few scrambling moves—almost. The next top, Mynydd Tal-y-mignedd is distinctive for its stone obelisk, built to celebrate Queen Victoria's Diamond Jubilee. From here the ridge continues as a broad grass plateau before a descent down broken slopes to Bwlch Dros-bern.

The next summit, Craig Cwm Silyn, marks the highest point of the traverse. A direct ascent provides an easy scramble similar in standard to that encountered on Mynydd Drws-y-coed. Easier lines avoiding the scramble lie to the right.

Although the highest point on the ridge, this is probably the least impressive summit—a broad rocky plateau reminiscent of the Glyderau. For impressive scenery you should head north to the edge of the plateau for a view of Craig Cwm Silyn, a popular rock climbing crag of huge proportions.

There are now three main options.

1. If you are walking the ridge as a linear route continue to the final summit of Garnedd Goch—an easy 2km/1¼ mile stroll across the plateau, the final stages beside a wall which leads directly to the summit (a useful landmark in poor visibility). From here head west to Cors y Llyn to finish near the village of Nebo.

2. If you intend to walk the ridge as a double traverse (both ways) the extra 4km/2½ mile out-and-back walk to Garnedd Goch will seem a waste of valuable energy and time. The true character of the ridge ends here. Retrace your steps back to Y Garn and descend to Rhyd-Ddu.

3. There are two options for a circular walk both using Bwlch-y-Ddwy-elor to return to Rhyd-Ddu but neither are particularly satisfying. The toughest but simplest is to return along the ridge to the western shoulder of Trum y Ddysgl and descend the broad grassy south ridge to the bwlch.

Alternatively, for less height gain, retrace your steps to Bwlch Drosbern, the last bwlch (directly below the east ridge of Craig Cwm Silyn). From here drop into the cwm to the south (right). Keep to the left-hand side of the stream and where this steepens into a small 'V'-shaped gorge curve leftwards into the adjacent cwm—Cwm Dwyfor.

There are mining remains in the bottom of the cwm here. Look for the bed of an old rail line where it passes through a crossing wall (GR. 541 503) and follow it as it contours out of the cwm and across the hillside. This can be overgrown and quite wet in places. In about 600m at GR. 545 498, and immediately after crossing a stream, turn left and head up through bracken on an indistinct path. At mines turn left up an old incline, then bear right with the path to continue the climb to Bwlch-y-Ddwy-elor.

From the bwlch a gate leads into the woods and a good path goes ahead through the trees. Eventually you reach a T junction. Turn right then left. At the next T junction turn left over a concrete bridge and turn right immediately onto a footpath beside the stream. At a crossing forest road take the path ahead, soon leaving the woods to traverse the lower slopes of Mynydd Drws-y-coed. At the path junction with the painted arrows on the rock passed earlier, keep ahead and retrace the outward journey.

Mynydd Tal-y-mignedd and Mynydd Drws-y-coed from Cwm Pennant

Mara Books

www.marabooks.co.uk/www.northerneyebooks.com

Mara Books publish a range of walking books for Cheshire and North Wales and have the following list to date. A complete list of current titles is available on our web site.

North Wales

Coastal Walks around Anglesey
ISBN 978 1 902512 20 4 *A collection of 22 circular walks which explore the varied scenery of Anglesey's beautiful coastline, designated an Area of Outstanding Natural Beauty.*

The Isle of Anglesey Coastal Path – The Official Guide
ISBN 978 1 902512 13 6. *A guide to the 125-mile circuit of Anglesey's stunning coast, an Area of Outstanding Natural Beauty.*

Walking in the Conwy Valley
ISBN 978 1 902512 11 2. *A collection of circular walks exploring the varied scenery of this beautiful valley from the Great Orme to Betws-y-Coed.*

Walking on the Lleyn Peninsula
ISBN 978 1 902512 15 0. *A collection of circular walks which explore both the wild and beautiful coastline and hills of the Lleyn Peninsula.*

Walking in the Clwydian Range
ISBN 978 1 902512 14 3. *A collection of 21 circular walks in the Clwydian Range Area of Outstanding Natural Beauty.*

Walking in Snowdonia Volume 1 – the northern valleys
ISBN 978 1 902512 06 8. *Twenty circular walks exploring the beautiful and dramatic valleys in the northern half of the Snowdonia National Park.*

A Pocket Guide to Snowdon
ISBN 978 1 902512 16 7. *A guide to every recognised route to the summit of Wales' highest mountain.*

Best Walks in North Wales

ISBN 978 0 9553557 3 8. *A colection of 28 circular walks ranged throughout North Wales, from the wilds of the Lleyn Peninsula through Anglesey and Snowdonia to the rolling hills of the Clwydian Range.*

The Mountain Men

ISBN 978 1 902512 11 2. *The story of the Victorian pioneer rock climbers active in Snowdonia up until the First World War.*

Cheshire

Circular Walks along the Sandstone Trail

ISBN 978 1 902512 21 1. *The Sandstone Trail is Cheshire's best known and most popular walking route. This book gives a complete route description along with 13 circular walks covering the entire trail.*

Walking Cheshire's Sandstone Trail

ISBN 978 0 9553557 1 4. *The official guide to Cheshire's premier walking route. The trail is described in both directions and is complemented by full colour photographs and Ordnance Survey mapping.*

Walks in Mysterious Cheshire and Wirral

ISBN 978 0 9553557 0 7. *A book of themed walks ranged throughout the county which focus on mysteries, folklore and legends.*

Walks in West Cheshire and Wirral

ISBN 978 0 9553557 2 1. *Thirty of the best walks in west Cheshire and Wirral.*

Circular Walks in Wirral

ISBN 1 902512 02 2. *A collection of circular walks in the coast and countryside of Wirral.*

Some common Welsh place name elements found in Snowdonia and their meaning:

Afon *(a-von)*.. *river*

Allt *(al-th-t)*.. *slope*

Bedd *(beth)*.. *grave*

Bwlch *(bul-k)*.. *pass*

Bychan *(buc-an)*.. *small*

Clogwyn .... *crag/cliff*

Crib/Gribin .... *ridge*

Cwm *(coom)*...................................... *glacial valley*

Ddu/Du *(thee, dee)*...................................... *black*

Ddysgl *(this-gul)*.. *dish*

Dyffryn .... *valley*

Fach/Bach *(vach)*.. *small*

Fawr/Mawr *(vaw-r)*.. *large*

Glas .... *green, blue*

Goch .... *red*

Graig/Craig .... *crag*

Gwastad .... *plain, level*

Llan .... *church*

Moel *(moy-l)*.............................. *bald or rounded hill*

Mynydd *(mun-uth)*...................................... *mountain*

Nant .... *stream*

Pen .... *head*

Rhyd .... *ford*

Saethau .... *to shoot, arrows*

Wen, gwyn .... *white*